AM I
BORING
MY DOG?

AM I BORING MY DOG?

AND 99 OTHER THINGS
EVERY DOG WISHES YOU KNEW

Edie Jarolim

ALPHA

A member of Penguin Group (USA) Inc.

ALPHA BOOKS

Published by the Penguin Group

Penguin Group (USA) Inc., 375 Hudson Street, New York, New York 10014, USA

Penguin Group (Canada), 90 Eglinton Avenue East, Suite 700, Toronto, Ontario M4P 2Y3, Canada (a division of Pearson Penguin Canada Inc.)

Penguin Books Ltd., 80 Strand, London WC2R 0RL, England

Penguin Ireland, 25 St. Stephen's Green, Dublin 2, Ireland (a division of Penguin Books Ltd.)

Penguin Group (Australia), 250 Camberwell Road, Camberwell, Victoria 3124, Australia (a division of Pearson Australia Group Pty. Ltd.)

Penguin Books India Pvt. Ltd., 11 Community Centre, Panchsheel Park, New Delhi—110 017, India

Penguin Group (NZ), 67 Apollo Drive, Rosedale, North Shore, Auckland 1311, New Zealand (a division of Pearson New Zealand Ltd.)

Penguin Books (South Africa) (Pty.) Ltd., 24 Sturdee Avenue, Rosebank, Johannesburg 2196, South Africa

Penguin Books Ltd., Registered Offices: 80 Strand, London WC2R 0RL, England

Copyright © 2009 by Edie Jarolim

International Standard Book Number: 978-1-59257-880-1
Library of Congress Catalog Card Number: 2009923300

11 10 09   8 7 6 5 4 3 2 1

Interpretation of the printing code: The rightmost number of the first series of numbers is the year of the book's printing; the rightmost number of the second series of numbers is the number of the book's printing. For example, a printing code of 09-1 shows that the first printing occurred in 2009.

Printed in the United States of America

For the rescuers, who rescue us, too, by bringing dogs into our lives, and for the first-time dog owners who've discovered it's never too late for puppy love.

CONTENTS

INTRODUCTION

"You're writing a book about dogs?" my friend Sharon asked, sounding surprised. "I never really thought of you as a dog person." Sharon and I have known each other since we were 5, so I wasn't surprised by her surprise. I never really thought of myself as a dog person either, until I got a dog, which made me a dog person by default. Before then, I was convinced there was a dog-person demographic—one that I didn't fit.

Not that I didn't like dogs. Far from it. But I grew up in pre-hip Brooklyn, with a mother who feared all creatures great and small. The dogs I saw on TV romped around the country-side or chased balls down suburban streets. They didn't board elevators in rundown apartment buildings or beg for pastrami from the corner deli. Nor did actual dogs frequent my early circles. The occasional hamster and odd budgie found their way into my friends' homes, but our childhood menageries were canine-free.

Marriage, tiny Manhattan quarters, graduate school, publishing jobs with long hours ... all, I decided, ruled out getting a dog. Even when I bought a house with a backyard in Tucson, Arizona, I remained dogless. Everyone knows that coyotes, not their domesticated kin, live in the desert.

Besides, I had become a travel writer.

I might have rationalized my prime dog-rearing years away, secretly worried that, like my mother, I lacked the canine caretaking gene. Then in 2004 I met Rebecca, fellow writer, fellow foodie—and evangelical dog rescuer.

The next thing I knew, I was palling around with terriers.

Or, to be specific, one small terrier mix: Frankie.

I didn't take Rebecca's canine bait right away, mind you. Sure, the picture she e-mailed me was cute, but Frankie was about 5 years old when he was found skittering around the streets of Tucson. I'd always pictured myself with a new model dog. And then there were my travels—not as frequent or far-flung as in the past, but still a good fallback excuse. What would happen to Frankie when I went away?

Rebecca informed me that older dogs were much mellower than puppies—and thus a better fit for a newbie like me—and that Frankie was very low maintenance. She promised to take care of him while I was gone, but pointed out that many hotels accept small dogs. The fact that I was always holed up, writing, when I was in Tucson was a real advantage, Rebecca added. She was certain I'd give Frankie a great home.

It was this last assurance that finally reeled me in. If a dog rescuer thought I'd be a good dog guardian ... well, maybe I would be.

And so, after deeming my home dog-safe (*Hint:* neatness is not a criterion), Rebecca asked me to suggest a date to begin Frankie's two-week trial stay with me. I optimistically chose my upcoming birthday.

I would like to report that Frankie and I bonded immediately, that as soon as his trusting little face looked into mine I knew I'd made the right decision. I would like to, but it would be a lie. Frankie's little face wasn't trusting; it was terrified. He glued himself to my couch and went on a hunger strike. His sole demand: Rebecca's return. I spent my birthday in tears, certain I'd made the biggest mistake of my life.

But pride and obstinacy have their rewards. I prefer not to admit that I've done something stupid (unless I'm certain to be found out, in which case I confess, all cheerful self-deprecation) or that I'm inept (ditto). I knew I was ignorant about all things canine, but I also knew that people far meaner than me managed to get dogs to like them. Surely I could win over one small, dejected pup.

I started calling friends and asking questions, reading dog books, going to training classes, asking more questions, reading some more. Frankie pitched in, after his desire for food overcame his ardor for Rebecca. And slowly, despite Frankie's fears and mine, we built a life together—a rich, complex, and frequently goofy one.

And that dog person profile? Feh. Anyone who likes dogs can—and deserves to—be a dog person. It's just a question of getting some basics under your belt.

Which is why I decided to write a book about dogs.

The result, *Am I Boring My Dog?*, is geared toward those who are contemplating getting a dog, those who have just gotten a dog, and those who believe they can do better by their dog—in short, the confused and the guilty. I remain among their vast ranks. I know a great deal more about dogs than I did before I got one and before I researched this book, but I learn something new each day. Frankie, in particular, lets me know that I still have a long way to go toward understanding his species—as, he believes, do animal scientists.

I'm not pleading ignorance as a disclaimer for anything I may have missed or gotten wrong (although I'd be very pleased to be excused for both). Rather, ignorance was at once an inspiration and a qualification for this project. People who grow up with dogs often don't know what they don't know. It's like the friend from California who came to visit me in New York and couldn't stop laughing when he discovered there was a neighborhood in Queens called Flushing. I'd gone through a childhood full of potty humor—including the entire I.P. line; remember *The Purple River* by I.P. Peculiar and *The Golden River* by I.P. Freely?—without ever noticing this fine local example.

Ignorance wasn't my only qualification for writing this book, however. As a travel journalist, I was charged with trying to make sense of foreign cultures—an excellent preparation for exploring Dog World. Looking back on my *Complete Idiot's Travel Guide to Mexico's Beach Resorts,* I've decided that Frankie is the Acapulco of dogs: charming, a bit older, but with fame that—I hope—is about to be burnished.

Getting a Ph.D. in literature turned out to be surprisingly useful, too. Compared with the writings of critics like Lacan and Derrida, even the most arcane of the many books I read by dog experts seemed lucid. My graduate school years at NYU also accustomed me to taking direction from a small, hairy creature, although Frankie is far handsomer—and considerably nicer—than my dissertation advisor was.

It turned out to be the best of times and the worst of times to decide to write a book about dogs. The current interest in all things canine suggests the existence of many potential book-buyers, which is excellent. But that interest also generated a vast amount of information that needed to be sifted through, much of it incorrect. (This includes the popular notion of dogs as furry children; children are, in fact, hair-challenged dogs.) Rather than risk data overload—and risk boring you, oh gentle book buyer—I outlined the basic issues, citing additional resources for those who want to explore them in greater depth.

For the same reasons, I've concentrated on first-dog—and therefore single-dog—households. You'll read about the importance of being a leader to your dog, for example, but not about introducing your second pup to your first. I've also resisted throwing too many humans into the mix. My prime focus is on the relationship between one person and one dog, with other people pretty much serving as support staff.

Frankie was naturally enlisted to illustrate many of the points I wanted to make. That's not to suggest any dog you get or already have will bear more than a superficial, species-based resemblance to him. You might even conclude that your dog is superior. Of course, you would be wrong.

A few words on terminology. I've used names of specific dogs (and people) whenever I knew them and wasn't writing anything that could be construed as libelous; dogs are notoriously litigious. Otherwise, I have alluded to "your dog," "pooch," "pup," and "canine" and—indiscriminately, but with the aim of equal time—used masculine and feminine personal pronouns. I've often observed the linguistic conventions of dogdom, including words like "poop" (which I never thought I'd hear from anyone other than parents of toddlers, much less use), but haven't always steered clear of disputed terms, such as "owner" as opposed to "guardian." Frankie is a rescue, which absolves me of any further need for political correctness.

In addition, I've sometimes made-up words—for example, dogdom—because it's my book and I can.

Finally, every advice book is expected to distill a bit of take-away wisdom. Here, then, are the top five things you need to do to maximize your dog's quality of life—and the quality of your lives together:

1. Feed your dog food (not too much).*

2. Provide plenty of exercise.

3. Train early and often.**

4. Spay or neuter your dog.

5. Don't support puppy mills.

---

* *With apologies—and thanks—to Michael Pollan (The Omnivore's Dilemma, In Defense of Food), whose warnings against unhealthy, overly processed food apply even more to the dog food made from the human variety's dregs.*

** *With thanks—and no apologies—to corrupt politicians, who provide us with nearly as much entertainment as dogs do. Let this also serve as a caution to ignore the book's footnotes at your peril. They're often as informative as—and frequently funnier than—the main text.*

Observing the first, second, and fourth rules will help maintain your dog's health; honoring the fourth and fifth will ensure you good karma; and following the second and third will go a long way toward keeping you from boring your dog. Which is only fair. Your dog may amuse you with his antics, amaze you with his wisdom, and, occasionally, fill you with fear or anguish, but he definitely won't bore you.

ACKNOWLEDGMENTS

Frankie, naturally, was my prime source of information and inspiration for this book, but many other dogs and their companion humans also contributed a great deal. The latter include Rebecca Boren, Frankie's rescuer, who remains a benevolent presence in our lives. Frankie is far less effusive toward Rebecca than he once was and than he should be, what with her saving his life and all, but—smart dog!—he doubtless wants to assure me of his undivided loyalty. He did indicate that he appreciated Rebecca's refurbishment of his favorite squeaky chile toy, albeit not directly to her.

Among the many other friends who contributed advice—almost always solicited—anecdotes, and general appreciation for dogs as well as for this project are (alphabetically): Barbara Buchanan, Lori Chamberlain, Kate Davis, Lydia Davis, Jennifer Duffy, Daniela Lax, Jean McKnight, Kathy McMahon, Elaine Raines, Kimberly Schmitz, Linda Snyder, and Karyn Zoldan. Their dogs are too numerous to thank—and, besides, prefer acknowledgment in edible form.

Although I rarely traveled during the writing of this book, it was nice to know I could depend on Linda Zubel and Sarah Meyer to take care of Frankie when I went on research trips, including attending the conference of the Association of Pet Dog Trainers in Louisville. The APDT professionals I met couldn't have been nicer to an outsider, and I learned a great deal about the efficacy of—and scientific basis for—kindness and fun as training techniques (in conjunction with consistency and firmness).

Dr. Randy Eberhardt earns kudos for being a skilled and wonderfully empathetic veterinarian. Where I allude to vets who said mean things about Frankie or subjected him to silly treatments, I am most definitely not referring to him.

I am grateful to Betty Liddick, editor of *Your Dog*, the newsletter of Cummings School of Veterinary Medicine at Tufts University, for encouraging my contributions and—after I paid my dues by taking on topics like shedding and inflammatory bowel disease—for giving me assignments that afforded me the opportunity to interview such top dog experts as Nicholas Dodman and Ian Dunbar.

Monte Workman, dog lover and artist extraordinaire, brought my text to life with his witty illustrations, and put up with my perfectionism.

Above all, I would like to thank Clare Macdonald, who appears frequently in these pages along with her wonder dog, Archie (formally, Archibald Macleash). Over the years, Clare's job description as my (human) best friend has often involved talking me down from feelings of unworthiness. By reading the manuscript and offering invaluable advice, she has helped make me—or at least my book—worthy.

CHAPTER 1

SO YOU THINK YOU WANT A DOG

1.   I'M CONTEMPLATING GETTING A DOG, BUT NEVER HAD ONE BEFORE. HOW DO I KNOW IF I'LL BE GOOD AT DOG CARE?

Concern and doubt are the hallmarks of today's dog owner, so you're not alone in wondering about your qualifications for the job. In the past few decades, dogs have joined babies as the objects of our obsessive attention—of intensive, often expensive, analysis. Whereas we once expected our furry friends to fend for themselves, psychologically speaking, we now fret over the angle and intensity of every tail wag and the volume and timbre of every bark.

Given all that pressure, the fact that you haven't mentioned renting a dog* is a good sign.

Relax. If you're responsible, ethical, reasonably solvent, and reasonably flexible, you can't fail to be a good dog guardian. You can and will make mistakes. But you will read, observe, seek advice, and learn. And you will never be mocked by your charge when you do something stupid.

In the end, you take a leap of faith. Dog is love.

2.   WILL GETTING A DOG CHANGE MY LIFE DRAMATICALLY?

Yes, and irrevocably—but in a good way. Unless you have a tiny, flinty heart, in which case you shouldn't inflict your mean self on a dog or any other living creature.

---

* *Rent-a-dog programs like FlexPetz have become so widespread that people concerned about animal welfare are working to get them banned. If you have trouble getting your head around the problem with renting a pet (even aside from the enforced puppy prostitution issue), think how you would view its application to those too busy to raise a child full time.*

3. I READ THAT AMERICANS SPENT MORE THAN $20 BILLION ON DOGS LAST YEAR. WHAT MAKES US SO GAGA ABOUT THEM?

Puppy love is no accident, nor does it stem from the efforts of a powerful dog lobby. Canine-human codependency has deep and ancient roots. Scientists haven't resolved precisely when and how dogs parted ways from wolves; most estimate that the process began more than 15,000 years ago. There's no question, however, that some canids discovered it was in their best interest to endear themselves to *homo sapiens* to get access to food and fires. Humans eventually became actively involved in the genetic selection process, breeding dogs to make them useful as well as appealing. Thus the bond between the two species developed and strengthened over time.

Interspecies communication is another matter, which I'll get to in Chapter 6; suffice it to say, it's nearly as complicated as intraspecies communication between the genders. One relevant example: dogs don't need much from us beyond the basics of food, shelter, and kind attention, rewarding us with intangibles like loyalty and devotion. Humans, in contrast, tend to confer pricey, often frivolous gifts on the objects of their affection—a display of status that dogs neither recognize nor respect.

4. WHAT'S THE BEST AGE AT WHICH TO GET A DOG?

When you're older than 45 and have given up on meaningful relationships with other humans.

Oh, you mean the dog.

It depends on your circumstances and temperament. Not everyone wants the hassle of housebreaking a puppy, or dealing with her irrational exuberance. Rescuing an older, mellower dog has its rewards, not the least of them knowing that you've saved an innocent from spending her golden years in the hound hoosegaw, perhaps on death row. Contrary to the tired maxim, you *can* teach old dogs new tricks. And there are no size surprises with a grownup.

In theory, raising a puppy will allow you to control the circumstances of his upbringing. But that's only true if you go to a reputable breeder who hasn't separated mother from offspring and sibling from sibling too early—just one of the innumerable bad practices of the mass breeding operations known as puppy mills that can lead to behavior problems later on. (See question 10 for more details.) And even the best attempts at socialization at the correct age and the most assiduous training can't guarantee you haven't brought home a bad seed (perhaps an overly inbred one) who will eventually manifest Cujo tendencies. Nor can you watch your pup 24/7. Control, as any shrink or Zen master will tell you, is impossible to achieve or merely an illusion.

So if I had to choose an ideal age at which to get a dog—who, in my ideal universe, would be housebroken and have no history of being mistreated—it would be about a year and a half for a small dog, two to two-and-a-half years for a larger one.* The pup has calmed down a bit but still has plenty of pizzazz—and, in most cases, plenty of years ahead to spend with you.

5. HOW DO I KNOW IF MY CHILD IS READY FOR A DOG?

If he or she is old enough to ask, that's a start—"ask" being the operative word. Never get a dog for a child who hasn't requested one just because you think he is lonely or needs to

---

* *Strange—and unfair—but true: In the canid kingdom, size counts when it comes to maturity. The larger the dog, the longer the maturation period but, perversely, the shorter the lifespan.*

learn responsibility. That would be the equivalent of using real babies rather than dolls or eggs in one of those teen anti-pregnancy programs that involves taking care of an infant for a week. Robotic dogs are now widely available, should such a lesson be your goal.

Then, take into account the circumstances that sparked the request. Wait at least three months after your child viewed the last dog movie, including animated ones (*101 Dalmatians* in any version is particularly dangerous). After that, you can consider it.

In the meantime, try not to be swayed by the intense desire to stop the cajoling and whining that tend to accompany all pet requests.* Inform your offspring that dogs are very sensitive to high-pitched sounds like whining, and that you couldn't possibly bring one into such an inhospitable environment.

Finally, ask yourself: Are you or anyone else in the family willing to take primary responsibility for the dog if your kid loses interest? If the answer is no, don't get a dog. It would not only be horribly unfair to the neglected pup, but also to the child, who'll come to associate dogs with nagging and yelling and, as a result, never want to have anything to do with the species later in life.

If you decide your household is truly dog-ready, involve your child in the adoption process, thereby ensuring a match of temperaments and creating an emotional bond. But avoid bringing a dog home during the holidays, a sure recipe for disaster. The excitement of the season leads to over-stimulation and bad behavior. The dog often gets really wound up, too.

That doesn't mean you shouldn't let your child associate getting a dog with the holidays, which is one way to ensure

---

* *A notable exception to this rule is Carly, a 10-year-old I know who gave a PowerPoint presentation to her parents to prove to them that she was dog worthy. Now there's a kid who earned her warm puppy!*

better memories of the season than most of us have. Either go together to get the dog in advance, stressing that this is a holiday gift, or give the child an IOU—perhaps tied to a stuffed animal—promising an excursion to get a pup in the new year. If your kid can't deal with the concept of advance or deferred gratification—or does really creepy things to the stuffed animal—then she isn't ready for a dog.

Whatever you do, avoid family trips to stores that sell puppies.* It's tough enough for a grownup to remember the greater good of shutting down puppy mills (see question 10) when faced with the pathos of a small, squirmy cutie in a cage. Don't expect your child to be able to grasp this difficult concept—or forgive you for dragging him away from that wagging tail.

6. SHOULD I GET A MIXED BREED OR A PUREBRED?

In the past, status in canine circles derived primarily from having a dog that conformed to the standards of a particular breed as defined by the American Kennel Club or United Kennel Club. Pejoratives like "mongrel" or "cur," which suggest a link between character and blood purity, were applied to dogs of unknown or mixed origin.

These days, because mixed breeds tend to be rescues more often than not, owning a mutt—even the term has acquired shabby chic cachet—confers a different type of status, that of moral superiority. So if you're disposed toward one-upmanship, you're no longer restricted to the breed-related variety—which clears the slate for criteria other than snobbery to be factored into your decision.

---

* Don't confuse getting a dog at a store like PetSmart, which holds fairs to find owners for rescued pets, with getting one through a shop that makes a business of selling animals. The price tags alone (see question 11) will tell you which is which.

PUREBRED PROS

- Predictability. If you're familiar with the dog's lineage, you have a pretty good idea what to expect with regard to size, temperament, and so on.

- You can aspire to appear on national TV in the Westminster Dog Show.

- You have a ready answer to the oft-posed question, "What kind of dog is that?"

PUREBRED CONS

- There's a reason that many states have laws against marriage between first cousins. Unfortunately, no similar statutes exist to muzzle doggie inbreeding. In particular, breeding for looks rather than temperament or athletic prowess has resulted in dogs that are predisposed to a variety of illnesses and afflictions, including, as a friend said about a breed that shall remain nameless, "heads so narrow that they have no room for brains."

- You might be mocked in a film such as *Best in Show*.

MIXED-BREED PROS

🦴   When people ask you what type of dog you have, you get to say stuff like "Heinz 57," "Pure speculation," or "Canardly." This last one is particularly entertaining if the questioner nods sagely and claims to have heard of a canardly instead of looking puzzled and waiting for the punch line, "I can hardly tell."

🦴   Fewer breed-related health problems.

🦴   The fun of blaming any undesirable traits on breeds you don't like, and claiming a lineage from breeds that you do. Caveat: To avoid seeming arbitrary or vindictive, you have to be reasonable about said blame and claim, staying within the realm of possibility as regards to size, color, and other physical attributes.

MIXED-BREED CONS

🦴   Unpredictable health problems.

🦴   Unpredictable size if you get the dog as a puppy. That adorable little Yorkie mix might turn out to have some German Shepherd in him. (And no, it's not impossible for two very divergent-size dogs to hook up. You'd be amazed what bitches in heat and the males who love them can do.)

7. GIVEN THE MORAL SUPERIORITY THAT RESCUING A DOG CONFERS, AM I A BAD PERSON FOR WANTING A PUREBRED?

No. Wanting a particular breed and wanting to rescue a dog are by no means mutually exclusive. According to the Humane Society of the United States, one of every four dogs in shelters is purebred. And the fact that they've been given up doesn't mean these pups are losers. Most dogs end up home-less because of circumstances that have little to do with them—including the sudden homelessness of their owners.

The website of the American Kennel Club lists rescue organi-zations for more than 150 breeds, some that you might never have heard of, like the Spinone Italiano (perhaps a cousin of the Gelato Hound); see www.akc.org/breeds/rescue.cfm. There are even rescue groups devoted to designer hybrids such as Puggles and Labradoodles. Ask your local shelter if they know of rescuers in your area that specialize in the breed you're seeking, and also check sites such as www.Pets911. com, www.Petfinder.org, 1-800-Save-A-Pet.com, and craigslist.com.

You're not a bad person either if you get a purebred from a breeder, as long as the breeder is reputable (see question 10).

If, however, you want a breed that matches your sofa and are likely to give the dog away after you redecorate your living room, then you *are* a bad person.

8. HOW MUCH CAN I EXPECT A PUREBRED TO COST?

Whatever the market will bear. You'll pay the most for dogs at the opposite ends of the popularity spectrum: the most sought-after and the rarest.

At a minimum, a "pet-quality" purebred—one that deviates from breed standards to the degree that it isn't considered dog show material—will run you $800, while "show-quality" pups start at about $1,500.

But that's the bottom line, and when dogs become trendy, expect to pay double the aforementioned prices—or more. Unscrupulous breeders bank on that, literally, rushing to supply dogs whenever the demand for them grows.

Of course, if you rescue a dog in the first place, you'll never pay more than the spay/neuter and veterinarian fees (see question 13).

9. HOW DO I FIND THE RIGHT BREED FOR ME/MY FAMILY?

Even if you're not the type to be swayed into getting a diminutive Mexican dog because you saw *Beverly Hills Chihuahua,* or a Bull Terrier because Budweiser's Spuds Mackenzie reminds you of your favorite uncle, emotion is bound to play a role in your breed choice nevertheless.

So step away from the computer, stop ogling pictures on Petfinder.com, and quit reading surveys on the best dog to get to attract members of the opposite sex or to promote a desired self-image. Instead, do some research into what your day-to-day life with an actual dog is likely to involve. The American Kennel Club's *Complete Dog Book* is a good place to start, but it doesn't cover all the negatives of health and temperament. Other books, including *The Perfect Match* by Chris Walcowicz and *Paws to Consider* by Brian Kilcommons and Sarah Wilson, are more honest about the downsides of various breeds.

As soon as you come up with some possibilities, look into whether there's a reputable breeder or breed rescue group near you. You might not get pedigreed puppies through a rescue group, but the advantage of going through one, even aside from the good karma, is that such groups are deeply invested in wanting to minimize returns and euthanizations. As a result, they'll evaluate you and your family situation carefully to determine whether a particular dog would be a good fit.

And always remember: dogs within any breed are individuals, even if they have the same parents. Think about it; are you and your siblings precisely alike? Are your offspring—other than identical twins—clones of each other?

With that caveat, here's a quick sketch of some breed groups you're likely to encounter in your research. They're based roughly on the categories established by the United Kennel Club (www.ukcdogs.com), which emphasize historic working roles more than the categories used by the American Kennel Club, which focus on appearance.

SPORTING DOGS: THE FIELD-AND-STREAM SET

Pointers, retrievers, setters, and spaniels—these are the sleek hunting dogs likely to turn up in an episode of *Masterpiece Theatre*. They generally require *lots* of exercise, and are especially fond of roaming off-leash, so if you want them to come back to you, you'll need to train them well. The retrievers, in particular, like to swim, so don't take them to the beach unless you're sure they won't keep going down the coast.

Note: The spaniels in this group are sometimes called Flushing Spaniels. This alludes to their ability to flush birds from their hiding places, not the ability to ensure themselves a fresh supply of water when they drink out of the toilet bowl.

HERDING DOGS: GET THEM DOGGIES ROLLIN'

We're talking Collies, Cattle Dogs, Sheepdogs, German Shepherds ... generally, anything with "sheep," "shepherd," or other types of livestock in their names (the Welsh Corgi is among the exceptions, both in its name and the length, or lack thereof, of its legs). No surprise: these pups like to round up and protect—and that means you, your kids, your other dogs, your cats ... If they can't get a herding gig, they'll settle for retrieving, so be prepared to do a lot of Frisbee throwing.

GUARD/PROTECTION DOGS: DON'T MESS WITH ME

Every flock requires not only a herder but also a guard to en-sure that there'll be livestock to herd, thus the ascent of such large, tough breeds as the Rottweiler, Doberman Pinscher, Great Dane, Boxer, and Saint Bernard. The biggest of the big, used as personal muscle for ancient warlords, often have "mastiff" in their names. This group tends to be smart and devoted, and members can be major sweetie pies, but they need to be shown who's paying their wages early on if you don't want them to lean on you.

THE NORTHERNERS: HAIRY AND HELPFUL

These big furballs, which include Akitas, Chow Chows, Mala-mutes, Huskies, and anything with "spitz" in their name, were assigned the same herding, hunting, and guarding tasks as the breeds already mentioned, only they performed them in the cold. No surprise, then, that they don't like vacation-ing in Florida or Arizona. They take their jobs seriously, and can be hard to handle without clear direction.

TERRIERS: NEVER SURRENDER

Airedale, Jack Russell, Scottish, Soft-Coated Wheaten ... having a dog with "terrier" as a surname is a dead giveaway that you're dealing with a feisty, high-energy pup. (Under-cover terriers include the Miniature Schnauzer and German Pinscher.) The smaller terriers were bred to get rid of rodents and vermin, which means they love to tunnel and dig. Mem-bers of this group tend to be endlessly amusing but very strong-willed. If you don't watch it, they'll have you trained to do their bidding in no time.

SIGHT HOUNDS: THE ARISTO-DOGS

Thin, elegant, graceful, and *fast*, this group includes Afghans, Greyhounds, Borzois, and Whippets. Although they're excel-lent hunters, they also tend to be gentle and sensitive; don't insult them or they'll take off in a flash. But these guys know how to relax when they're not on the clock; around the house, they're quintessential couch potatoes.

SCENT HOUNDS: AIN'T NOTHIN' BUT A ...

In contrast to the upscale sporting dogs, these hunters—they include the Bloodhound, Beagle, and Coonhound—often get roles in films like *Deliverance*. Because they keep their noses close to the ground to track their quarry, many of them have short legs (badgers were once the Dachshund's specialty). They're used to running in packs, and are happy to have your family serve that role, but have a tendency to bark and howl, the better to let you know they've treed some creature—or would like to. Initial training should take place inside the house; when outside, these dogs are easily distracted by all those exciting scents.

COMPANIONS: HONEY, I SHRUNK THE DOG

Of course, it's not only small pups that make good pals; indeed, most of the toys—among them the Chihuahua, Maltese, Pekingese, Papillon, Pug, Miniature Poodle, and Yorkshire Terrier—originated in one of the other breed groups. It's just that these portable pets never really had another job description besides "go forth and be adorable," so nap snuggling is a task at which they excel. Don't let their cuteness deter you from serious training, however; small dogs that follow their own inclinations can be just as annoying as their larger counterparts, if somewhat less capable of doing major damage.

A few other variables that transcend breed include the following.

LONG-TERM COST

A large dog doesn't necessarily have more energy or need more exercise than a small one. There's no question, however, that the size of your grocery bill will be directly proportional to the size of your dog. In addition, some dogs are more likely than others to incur high vet costs. Boxers, for example, are prone to heart disease and gastrointestinal ailments, while German Shepherds are subject to hip dysplasia.

Sometimes these two cost categories overlap—many large dogs have a tendency to ingest undigestible items that require surgical removal. For example, Schatzi, a sweet Bernese Mountain dog I know, likes to eat tennis balls, pantyhose, and beach towels, among other items. These omnivore tendencies—which her owners have tried to anticipate and head off, to no avail (see "Intelligence," in the later section)—have already landed Schatzi in the doggie ER twice.

COAT

There are two types of allergies to consider when it comes to a dog's coat: an allergy to fur and an allergy to vacuuming. Double-coated dogs such as those in the Northern group sometimes shed the equivalent of another dog. In contrast, Poodles, Cairn Terriers, and the hairless Chinese Crested are among the dogs that are unlikely to make you sneeze—or clean.

INTELLIGENCE

Naturally, you want a really smart pup, right? Maybe—and maybe not. Intelligence is not necessarily the most desirable trait to seek in a dog. As with really smart people, high IQ pups can be high maintenance; not only will they figure out how to open your refrigerator and eat last night's pot roast, but after they do so they'll want to know what's next on the agenda. They often get bored easily. In contrast, some canines that never make the dean's list may be appealingly mellow. And after you get them to catch on to the connection between the peculiar vocalizations you're making and the behavior you expect from them, they're happy to go along with your program. According to Stanley Coren in the *Intelligence of Dogs*, out of 79 evaluated, the breeds that rank highest in the "working intelligence" category are the Border Collie, Poodle, German Shepherd, Golden Retriever, and Doberman Pinscher. The Borzoi, Chow Chow, Bulldog, Basenji, and Afghan have been relegated to the brains basement.

10. YOU'VE MENTIONED PUPPY MILLS SEVERAL TIMES. HOW DO I AVOID THEM AND FIND A RESPONSIBLE BREEDER?

As defined by the ASPCA, a puppy mill is any large-scale commercial breeding operation where profits are given a higher priority than the dogs' well-being. Although they've only recently begun to get widespread and well-deserved censure, these mass puppy producers have been around since the 1960s, when the demand—fed by franchises that realized putting adorable doggies in the window was the best way to draw people in to buy pet supplies—began outstripping the supply. Today, about 5,000 such operations, many on farms in the Midwest and Pennsylvania formerly devoted to raising pigs and chickens supply many of America's pet stores.*

These stores and boutiques, which tend to be in upscale malls or posh neighborhoods, hide the (often literally) dirty secret of the origins of their cute customer magnets. Puppy mills or factories have been found crowding some 1,000 dogs into

---

* About five years ago—not coincidentally, around the time that U.S. authorities started investigating unsavory breeders at home—puppy mills began cropping up in foreign countries. Mexico currently supplies many of California's pet boutiques with bootleg pups, and Russia and South Korea are among the countries flying mass-produced dogs to a variety of U.S ports with forged proof of rabies vaccination and of age (the minimum age for import is six months, but many puppies are flown in at six weeks).

facilities that are at best sterile and devoid of opportunities for social contact but far more frequently unsanitary and cruel.

But the puppies at least have to *look* healthy to be salable, although many have genetic defects based on bad breeding practices, not to mention diseases spread by overcrowding. The conditions under which the breeding mothers literally labor are far worse. Many of these dams, whom the public never sees, spend their entire lives in wire cages stacked one on top of the other, and left in cold, dark sheds. Because it costs more to secure the services of a vet than to get a new dog to push out puppies, sick mothers are often left to starve to death when they outlive their usefulness. Sometimes this occurs even when the dogs aren't sick but when a particular breed goes out of fashion.

Feeling upset enough yet? Here's more: Most of these doggie gulags are completely legal. They operate under the same USDA regulations applied to farm animals slated to be killed and consumed—except that, when the livestock consists of puppies, even fewer inspectors are assigned to ensure that conditions are even minimally humane.

Pet stores aren't the only places that purvey canine unfortunates.* Beware of ads in local giveaway papers and vendors hawking "purebred" puppies on street corners. True, the *Penny Saver* advertisers and sidewalk hawkers may only be backyard breeders—as amateurs looking to make a buck off their best friends are known—as opposed to puppy mill operators trying to get around the bad press and lemon laws associated with selling their wares through pet stores. But in neither case do you get a guarantee of the health or temperament of the dogs being sold, nor verifiable information on the conditions under which they've been raised.

---

* *They are, however, the only ones subject to the "pet lemon laws" that several states have passed. Statutes vary, but at the least they're designed to compensate buyers for veterinarian bills incurred to treat puppies that turn out to be sick.*

These days, the Internet is a major source of mass-produced puppies. Shady dog vendors keep few records, but it's a good bet that virtual sales are catching up with, if not outpacing, brick-and-mortar transactions. You'd be surprised how many people are taken in by slick-looking websites, sending money for long-distance pets without even requesting references. I'm not sure which is worse—actually receiving a puppy mill graduate who might be seriously ill and break your heart as well as your bank account, or wiring money to Nigeria and getting no dog at all.

Which brings me to the question of how to find a reputable breeder. Because one of the things that makes breeders reputable is their focus on one or, at the most, two breeds—thus allowing them to acquire in-depth knowledge of everything from standard appearance and temperament to health problems—you first need to decide on the breed you're interested in. In addition, attending local dog shows and agility trials sanctioned by the American Kennel Club or the United Kennel Club is a good way to check out different types of dogs in action and to meet breeders. However, these shows—which are not held in every town—don't give you the chance to make the acquaintance of less peppy and performance-oriented pups.

After you decide on a breed, seek referrals through friends, veterinarians, groomers, and through the AKC or UKC; these last two groups offer comprehensive lists of good breeders throughout the United States. Make sure to look for someone within easy visiting distance, because no matter how much you trust a referral, you'll want to check out a breeder's premises personally.*

---

* *There's also the issue of transportation if you consider someone who's not a reasonable drive from you. Some breeders claim they prepare their puppies in advance for the experience of being shipped by plane to avoid having them stressed by their journey. What do you imagine preparation for a stay in a plane's luggage hold might involve—keeping the little guy crated in a dark, airless room for indefinite periods of time without letting him go to the bathroom? Do you really want a puppy that's been doubly traumatized—assuming that the claim of preparation is even true?*

When you've found some promising possibilities, let the scrutiny begin.

PHASE 1: WEEDING OUT THE SEEDY BREEDERS

Before making a trip to visit the premises, ask the following questions.

Do you always have puppies available?

This is a trick question. An affirmative answer suggests that mama dog is kept bare-pawed and pregnant more frequently than is good for her health. Once-a-year breeding is ideal; more than twice borders on abuse. Good breeders keep a list of interested buyers to contact when the next litter is available.

A corollary of this question is "How soon after he's born can I get the puppy?" Be suspicious of any breeder willing to separate a puppy from dam and siblings before eight weeks at a minimum.

Will I be able to meet the parents of my puppy so I can get a sense of the offspring's appearance and temperament?

There's no reason you shouldn't be able to make the mother's acquaintance. If the father can't be present—and you're within your rights to ask why not—request to see documents proving that poppa has been registered with the AKC or UKC. (Beware of someone who says that they've got documentation from, say, the Siberian Kennel Club—even if you're looking at Siberian Huskies.)

Can you provide references from a local vet and from families who have purchased puppies from you?

Be sure to follow up with them all if for no other reason than that it's fun to chat with fellow admirers of the breed to hear about the joys—and travails—of bringing up the pups.

What potential health problems is the breed subject to?

This is another trick question. If the breeder answers "none," that's a sign of either ignorance or dishonesty. All breeds are predisposed toward certain health problems; good breeders work diligently to avoid them. You need to know how severe any inherited condition might be and—more important— whether a puppy from a litter you're contemplating has in fact inherited it.

If you decide to get a puppy from a breeder, it's completely kosher to request documentation from the Orthopedic Foundation for Animals (www.offa.org)—an organization devoted to reducing the incidence of a wide range of genetic diseases—that the parents and grandparents have been tested and shown to be defect free.

PHASE 2: PEERING AROUND THE PREMISES

Assuming a breeder has passed these preliminary pup quizzes, it's time to head out to see how the dogs are kept. If a breeder has a problem with your visiting when no puppies are available, then you have a problem with the breeder.

Look for the following.

Do the dogs you encounter seem healthy, upbeat, and friendly toward strangers?

If they slink off or bark frantically, you might consider slinking off, too.

Where do the dogs stay? Are they allowed indoors and kept in clean, well-maintained areas, or are they confined in smelly outdoor pens? Do they have sufficient room for exercise?

Or, in short, is this a place you wouldn't wish on a dog.

Does the breeder use harsh methods to make the dogs behave?

A well-behaved dog doesn't necessarily mean a happy dog, just one that's toed the line. I have no idea if stress hormones have an impact on the development of puppies (though why wouldn't they?); I just wouldn't want to buy a dog from a mean breeder.

PHASE 3: GETTING TO KNOW ME

A breeder should be interested in you, too, not just in your money.

Some signs that the well-being of the dog is foremost to the breeder:

- Multiple, relaxed visits are encouraged with your entire family.

- You're asked why you want a dog and who in the family will be responsible for her daily care.

- You're required to provide proof from your landlord or co-op board that you're allowed to have a dog (if you live in a building like the one where I used to live in Manhattan, you should be asked for verification that the puppy has personally passed muster with the co-op board).

- If you already have another dog, you're asked for references from a vet.

PHASE 4: ASSESSING THE LITTER

This is perhaps the toughest phase because actually viewing puppies is bound to cloud your ability to think clearly. Nevertheless, try not to be swayed by their overwhelming cuteness and consider the following.

Are the puppies kept with their mothers and siblings—and encouraged to interact with humans, too?

Duking it out for position with other dogs, being handled by humans, and being introduced to a variety of stimuli—all part of the process known as socialization—are essential to a well-balanced dog.

PHASE 5: BRINGING HOME BABY

When you're ready to take your new puppy home you should expect ...

> A written contract that you will return the dog if you can't keep her (see question 14). Unless you get a show-quality dog, the contract is likely to include an agreement that you will spay or neuter him.

> Records of veterinary visits for the puppy, a detailed explanation of her medical history, and a clear list of what vaccinations she will need and when.

> Assurances that advice on the care and feeding of your new friend will be available when you need it.

No, a breeder isn't required to be on call at all hours like a pediatrician, but one who cares about dogs will want to help you succeed in your new responsibilities, which can be overwhelming initially.

11. WHAT ABOUT MIXED BREEDS—AREN'T THE PROBLEMS OF FINDING THE RIGHT DOG COMPOUNDED WHEN YOU RESCUE A MUTT?

Quite the opposite. All but the most reputable breeders are solely in the dog business for the money, whereas shelters and rescue organizations (see the following question) are in it for the love—which means that their only motive is to ensure that their charges find good homes. As a result, most do their best to assess each animal's temperament before sending them off to be adopted; many offer adoption counseling. And with mixed breeds, you have the added advantage of being free from preconceptions, so the pup's actual personality isn't obscured by breed stereotypes.

Evaluating dogs and their potential guardians—on an individual basis—is the premise of the excellent Meet Your Match (MYM) program being introduced into more and more shelters, with the goal of determining whether you and a particular dog are suited for one another. A kind of interspecies Match.com, MYM evaluates the dogs' behavior, then categorizes them by character traits like "wallflower," "free spirit," or "teacher's pet." A potential adopter fills out a short form that serves as a canine personality wish list—and voilà, a love connection that's based on more than just looks. Developed by Emily Weiss, DVM, and sanctioned by the ASPCA, this program has greatly increased adoptions in the shelters that have used it—and cut back on returns.

Sadly, not all shelters have the funding and the staff to institute these types of programs or even to do detailed evaluations. In these cases, an excellent alternative is to hire your own matchmaker: a trainer. Good trainers (see Chapter 6 for advice on finding them) are especially well equipped for the task because they work with difficult-to-handle humans on a regular basis. Thus they are capable of not only assessing the temperament of dogs at the pound but also of talking potential adopters down from emotional reactions such as "he's so sweet" or "she'd make such a good hiking companion" if the dog that elicits it doesn't fit their lifestyle (or apartment).

Then there's the dumb luck factor. Full disclosure: Faced with appealing photographs and persuasive dog rescuers, my best (human) friend Clare and I eschewed the painstaking research I'm advocating here and took the blind emotional route. And we couldn't be crazier about our furry gentlemen friends, Archie and Frankie.

12. ARE THERE DIFFERENT TYPES OF SHELTERS—AND DOES IT MATTER WHICH ONE I VISIT TO FIND A DOG?

Sometimes called "pounds" because they once housed only impounded animals, shelters vary in everything from their admission and euthanization policies,* medical services, and outreach programs to the size and cleanliness of their facilities. No centralized agency exists to set guidelines or even to collect data about them. Strange but true: shelters with names that include "SPCA" or "Humane Society" have no affiliation with the Humane Society of the United States or with the American Society for the Prevention of Cruelty to Animals. The ASPCA does operate one shelter, in Manhattan, but it and the HSUS are primarily educational organizations, not governing or funding bodies.

The care of homeless or displaced dogs falls to three basic types of organizations.

MUNICIPAL SHELTERS

These are government-owned and -operated and thus funded by state, county, city, or township tax dollars. They typically come under the aegis of health care or law enforcement departments. Historically created to protect people from animals, they often do the opposite these days. If, for example, they're supervised by law enforcement, police officers may

---

* Some shelters keep dogs for only a week or two before they euthanize them; others hold onto them until they are adopted. But it's a complicated issue, so don't be quick to judge. A shelter that calls itself "no-kill," for example, may not accept animals who are unlikely to be adopted, or may euthanize those that become sick or exhibit behavioral problems. And if a shelter's facilities are inadequate and its adoption rates are low, who's to say whether a quick death wouldn't have been kinder than indefinite incarceration?

bring in dogs that have been abused—as well as those who've bitten neighborhood children (often one and the same pup). You can generally recognize municipal shelters by such utilitarian phrases in their names as "Animal Control" or "Animal Service."

PRIVATE NONPROFIT SHELTERS

The only thing that these shelters have in common is that they're designed to protect animals from people—or from the elements—and that they don't make money by doing so. They may get some funding from municipal contracts or may operate solely on the basis of private donations, large and small.

RESCUE GROUPS

These informal, privately funded organizations work with both municipal and private shelters, as well as with individuals who surrender their dogs. They may have a physical facility but more typically they keep the dogs they save from euthanization in foster homes or kennels.* Many focus on a single breed and may therefore operate under the auspices of a breed club. However, because the goal of most rescue groups is to find good homes for as many dogs as possible, they aren't always terribly strict about their categorizations.

For example, Frankie's rescuer, Rebecca, was affiliated with Arizona Mini-Schnauzer Rescue. Although Frankie shows no signs of Schnauzer—mini or maxi—parentage, Rebecca fostered him anyway because she's kind-hearted and Arizona Cute Fuzzy Dogs of Indeterminate Origin Rescue doesn't exist. I shudder to think that Frankie might have been executed because of breed profiling—or lack thereof.

All this may matter little to you as a potential adopter, especially if you find your dog through the Internet—where

---

* *Some are simply hoarders, but I'd rather focus on the majority of terrific people who do tireless, often thankless, work than on pathological pet collectors.*

shelters and rescue groups post their resident pups on sites such as Petfinder.com—and you only go to the shelter to retrieve her. But if you're doing a search in person, it's useful to know a shelter's euthanization policy. You may not be comfortable going to a place where you'll need to make a quick adoption decision—or, on the other hand, you may want to have urgency imposed because you're a ditherer. And if you discover that your local shelter doesn't have the resources to do temperament evaluations, you'll know that you need to bring an expert along.

But the dogs are equally worthy at every facility. And after you've settled in with your pound pup, you can decide at leisure which shelter or rescue group deserves your donations and/or can best benefit from your volunteer efforts.

13. IF RESCUING A DOG IS A GOOD DEED, WHY DO I HAVE TO PAY A FEE AND HAVE SOMEONE INSPECT MY PLACE?

To prove that you're not going to use your new pal as bait in a dog-fighting ring. Many people give away dogs with the best of intentions—and the best of results. But pups offered gratis to complete strangers too often end up in bad situations.

And if you can't find the money to make the (generally) required contribution to a shelter, then you probably can't afford to feed and care for a dog, either. Fees are usually considerably less than they would be for the same exam and neutering/spaying procedure done privately because many vets volunteer their services at local shelters. You're unlikely to have to come up with more than $200 initially.

Not all rescue groups have time to do home inspections, but many require them, so don't get insulted if someone wants to come check out your house. And don't worry. The nice folks at the shelter want to make sure that your adoptee is not going to escape through that big hole in your fence and find himself homeless again. They are not, as I had assumed, judging your décor, your cleaning skills, or your domestic arrangements (unless these include living with two dozen cats—or children—and/or with a burly rifle-wielding person). While I waited for my dog's rescuer to come over to evaluate the suitability of my house, I fretted that she would think it wasn't tidy enough. If you want proof that I knew next to nothing about dog rescue before I got Frankie, there you have it in a nutshell.

That said, rescuers and fosterers have been known to make unreasonable demands on potential pet owners for a variety of reasons that all boil down to "bad human, bad human!" If you like a dog and are uncertain of the appropriateness of an inspector's requirements, call the organization you're working with and ask for clarification.

14. WHAT IF I GET A DOG WHO DOESN'T LIKE ME?

This question will only seem odd to people who have had a chance to get acquainted with their new pals before bringing them home. If, as I did, you fall for a picture that a dog rescuer e-mails you, it's not an altogether irrational concern.

Rebecca, the aforementioned dog rescuer and fosterer, had told me that Frankie was sweet natured, which was true. Not having had the opportunity to observe his behavior long-term, however, she couldn't know that he was a one-person pup, a canine serial monogamist. During the tour of my house, Frankie shadowed Saint Rebecca, avoiding me like I was a large, unpredictable predator. When it became clear that she was about to take off without him, he looked at her piteously, silently imploring, "Don't leave me here. She's clueless."

Nor did things improve soon. For the first few days, Frankie lay on the couch, languishing, a tiny furry Camille. I became convinced that he hated me, that, as I'd feared, I was an abject failure at dog ownership.

This story has a happy ending, if you consider having an 11-pound alien take over your life a happy ending. Frankie now adores me (and only me). As a result, I am entirely at his disposal.

But I only gave the little guy a chance because I knew that I could—indeed, was required to—give him back if things didn't work out. My adoption contract, typical of most, reads: "I agree that if at any point I cannot keep the animal, I will return him/her to the original rescue without requesting a fee." This stipulates no time limit and provides no definition of "cannot keep the animal," which can thus be construed to mean "because he hates me and refuses to get off the couch."

The bottom line: Don't get a dog from a rescue group or breeder who says you can't return him, unconditionally (although not uncommunicatively; you *do* need to explain what went wrong so that a shy couch-hugger isn't mistaken for an aggressive teeth-sinker). But that doesn't mean you should regard the adoption process as akin to shopping at Nordstrom. People who are serial and frivolous returners—most puppies *will* chew on shoes; you can't keep trying to find one who's allergic to leather—you'll quickly become known on the shelter gossip circuit as someone who should be refused a dog.

15. WHY SHOULD I GET A DOG RATHER THAN A CAT?

- A dog won't make you feel like a slob. A cat's hyper-fastidiousness serves as a constant rebuke to those of us with messy tendencies. In contrast, you're bound to feel neat in comparison with a pet that likes to roll around on dead pigeons.

- A dog won't ignore you. He may irritate you with demands for attention or with his attentions to you, but you'll never feel as though you're on the needy end of a romantic relationship.

- If you're female and single and have a cat—especially more than one—you run the risk of being regarded as a cliché when you pass the age of 30.*

- If you're male and single and straight, sharing your home with a cat may lead others to question your masculinity. Multiply that doubt by the number of cats you have.*

---

* *I'm referring here only to an either/or situation. If you can manage to comingle cats, dogs, fish, and ferrets, you'll be regarded as very open and inclusive (not to mention as very busy at mealtimes and cleanups). But there's a fine line. Unless you live on a farm or a ranch, having more four-legged creatures than rooms in your home can lead others to doubt your sanity—and your sanitation standards.*

🦴   A cat won't allow you to dress him or to pose him in front of a bowling alley or a drum set.

🦴   Being accompanied by a dog will allow you to talk aloud to yourself in public without appearing crazy (or obnoxious, as would be the case if you were attached to a cell phone). *Caveat:* If you act as though your dog is answering you, then you will seem crazy anyway.

🦴   By obeying selected commands, dogs let you maintain the illusion that you have power over them. Cats don't bother to pretend that they don't rule your life.

🦴   If you die on his watch, a dog will remain by your side, waiting for you to wake up and feed him. A cat will just feed on you.*

---

* *Yes, dogs may eventually eat their owners rather than starve (just as some Donner Party members dined on their pals), but they wait far longer than cats, who transform their caregivers into a food source in just a day or so. And some dogs will die of starvation rather than be disloyal. Have you ever heard of a cat doing that?*

CHAPTER 2
HE'S NEARLY HERE—
NOW WHAT?

16. WHAT'S THE MINIMUM I SHOULD GET BEFORE I BRING MY DOG HOME?

Puppies and adult dogs have slightly different needs, but the essentials are the same: food, shelter, basic cable (okay, entertainment). Your needs, in contrast, tend to center around keeping your new pal from escaping and/or destroying stuff.

To those ends, you'll want to lay in the following:

- Bedding
- A collar and ID tags (see also question 23)
- A leash and, in some cases, halter
- Food, including treats
- A few safe toys
- One bowl for food, one for water
- A crate
- A baby gate (if you need to cordon off a separate room for the dog to stay)*
- Cleaning supplies, especially those meant to soak up odors
- List of emergency numbers
- Recreational substance of choice (for you, not the dog)

I'll go into detail about most of these items in later chapters. But except for investing in high-quality food** and a decent crate for an adult dog, don't, I repeat, don't, spend much money on any of them. Clean towels or blankets make good

---

* These are less expensive than—and as effective as—their canine equivalents unless your dog weighs more than 50 pounds.

** Also lay in a small quantity of the food your dog is accustomed to—assuming you know—so you can ease her into a new culinary plan rather than shocking her system.

temporary beds for dogs who may not have their bathroom habits under complete control. Your pooch won't be impressed by the glaze on an expensive ceramic bowl, and you'll only be irritated if she's not interested in—or quickly demolishes—that pricey stuffed bear. Besides, you'll discover that after you get a dog, your friends will buy gifts for her instead of for you. Let them shell out the money for the good stuff.

Some experts recommend buying a toothbrush and grooming tools, including nail clippers, to get your dog accustomed to his toilette right off the bat. I think it's okay to allow him some lapses in personal hygiene for a few weeks, until he gets to know and trust you a bit. (I draw the line at a dog that's rolled in something disgusting, in which case a prompt shampooing is called for.)

17. HOW ELSE SHOULD I PREPARE FOR THE HOMECOMING?

Meditate. Play racquetball. Watch dumb movies. Do whatever it is you usually do to relax (except for drinking heavily; you've got too much to accomplish). Both you and your new dog are going to be under a good deal of stress initially; accept that and try to minimize it.

Along with your personal chilling techniques, it's useful to ...

CLEAR SOME SPACE (LITERALLY)

Many dogs, especially those who've been kept in a small area in a shelter, aren't used to their new-found freedom and get nervous if they're allowed to wander freely right away. And many have a tendency to, well, dog you wherever you go. Being shadowed is very unnerving if you're not used to it—and even if you are. So clear out a space that your dog can settle into and explore safely and that you can easily clean—maybe the kitchen if it's large enough. Exploring can come later; for the time being, there's security in containment for both of you.

Limiting the range of exploration will also allow you to determine just how much damage your dog is capable of inflicting on your house. Puppies can be depended on to try to ingest pretty much everything, so be sure to put breakables and electric cords out of reach, and to apply a safe (both for the furniture and the dog) antichew substance such as bitter apple to the wooden legs of any item that can't be relocated without difficulty.

CLEAR SOME SPACE (METAPHORICALLY)

There's a fine line between socializing a puppy and terrifying him. Don't isolate your dog but don't overwhelm him either. Feed him, hang out with him, take him outside, let him know you're around—but don't crowd him. If your dog is outnumbered by humans in your household, have each family member approach individually rather than en masse.

DON'T GET HUNG UP ON DETAILS

What I remember most vividly about Frankie's first days with me was feeling overwhelmed. Well-meaning friends would recommend the best places to shop for inexpensive flea and tick medication while I was struggling with the big picture: that there was an alien creature in my house who didn't appear to like me. Arrange to have a calm, dog-savvy friend on call who will address all your concerns, no matter how trivial, but who will not offer unsolicited advice.

In my case, it turned out to be my friend Elaine—as I discovered when I phoned her in a panic because half of Frankie's morning poop production was stuck, drying, to his rear end. I couldn't imagine trying to clear off the mess with shampoo, but didn't believe either Frankie or I would appreciate its presence for very long. Elaine advocated an immediate application of toilet paper to remove as much of the offending matter as possible—and then explained that sometimes you need to give your dog's butt a haircut. She didn't proceed to tell me that PetSmart was having a kibble sale.

PLAN TO BE AT HOME FOR AT LEAST TWO DAYS

This is key, whether you're paper training a puppy or trying to make an older dog feel comfortable. If various family members are to be assigned different doggie responsibilities, get them sorted out during this period. But setting aside two days to get acquainted doesn't mean you should never leave the house. This is a great time to set the tone for your departures. Going out for increasingly long periods (though not more than a few hours) without making a fuss—that's right, no dramatic farewells—will prepare your dog for your future absences while assuring him of your dependable eventual return.

FIND A TRAINING CLASS

Puppies should be socialized and taught good manners as soon as possible, so don't wait to locate a good trainer—which I discuss in Chapter 6—for yours. But older dogs need education, too. The sooner you rid them of behaviors that bother you, the happier you'll both be.

GET READY TO HANG ON—AND ENJOY THE RIDE

You'll almost certainly be on an emotional rollercoaster when a dog enters your life. One minute she'll do something amusing like licking your knee, and you'll think, "I love her. She's a hoot!" The next, she'll start barking furiously at nothing, and you'll decide you were insane to take on this responsibility. Mood swings are perfectly normal and they'll subside—at least for long stretches of time.

18. WHAT'S THE BEST WAY TO BRING MY DOG HOME?

This is not as obvious as you might think. Unless you live within walking distance of a shelter or a breeder, an automobile is likely to be involved. But whose automobile? You might want to use your own car so as to introduce your dog to his future chariot right off. Then again, you might want to borrow a car from a good friend or close family member, so that any trauma associated with the trip home isn't revisited every time your dog sees your vehicle.

If your dog isn't used to a crate and, especially, a crate small enough to serve as a carrier, bringing him home in captivity isn't the best way to roll out the welcome mat.* For puppies and small dogs, a towel-lined cardboard box—or a designated hugger—is a far better option. You'll therefore need the aforementioned friend or family member to accompany you, either to do the driving or to sit in the backseat with your pup.

It's only fair to make potential dog attendants aware that, besides calming duties, they may be expected to perform such functions as keeping your dog from leaping into the front seat and cleaning up any messes created by nervousness or carsickness, canine or human. For the latter reason, it's a good idea to cover the car's backseat with old towels or sheets before embarking on this adventure; to take along a roll of paper towels for mop-ups; and to crack the car windows sufficiently to provide air—but not enough to allow escape, canine or human.

---

* If you're considering a car service or taxi, a dog carrier might be your best bet. Or lying. That is, if you don't want to use a carrier but don't want the cabbie to know your fellow passenger is a new, untested pup, muster all your moxie to pretend you've been traveling with this dog all your life—and hide the emergency cleanup towels in a bag from an upscale department store.

19. WHAT SHOULD I CALL MY DOG?

Call him anything you like—just don't call him late for dinner.

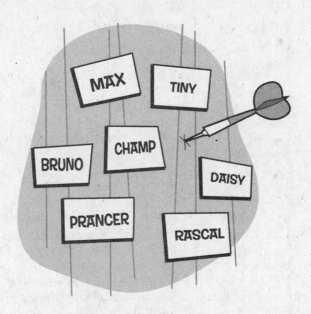

Hold the groans. It happens to be true, at least from your dog's perspective. Unlike children, who grow up to resent you if you saddle them with embarrassing monikers, dogs don't care what sounds you use to summon them. In fact, if you need to change your pup's name down the road,* you can do so over the course of a few days by plying him with treats and other signs of approval.

Humans, on the other hand, attach great significance to names, which are also key to communicating with and training your dog. So it's in all your best interests to decide on something suitable as soon as possible.

---

* This should only be done under duress—if, say, you're moving in with someone who has the same name as your dog. When you change names too often, you run the risk of your dog ignoring all summonses—and of becoming obese as a result of repeated retraining programs.

You'll have plenty of help. Entire books have been devoted to dog names, replete with etymologies. Forget Fido, Spot, and Rover. According to a Dogster.com survey, the most common labels for today's trendy pup are the following:

For girls: Lucy, Bella, Daisy, Molly, Maggie, Chloe, Sophie, Lola, Bailey, Roxy.

For boys: Buddy, Max, Jake, Charlie, Rocky, Jack, Bailey, Toby, Buster, Bear.

I'm sorry to report that Lucky also ranks rather high on both the male and female lists—sorry because vets agree that Lucky may be the unluckiest name ever to grace a dog collar. To use it is to invite disaster.*

Trends notwithstanding, it's best to find a name that fits the personality and appearance of the actual dog who has taken up residence with you.

Trying out different names on puppies is easy. They're too busy figuring out the relationship between piddling on the carpet and the loud vocalizations the act elicits to worry about any less urgent noises being directed toward them. But don't worry about creating an identity crisis in an adult dog that you adopt from a shelter, either; except under rare circumstances, your new pup is already operating under an assumed—or rather, newly assigned—name (the ability to respond to which may be among the things that saved her life). Nevertheless, it's still best to audition new names surreptitiously until you're certain you have a winner.

Along with sussing out the suitability of a name to your new pal's looks and personality, there are some other factors to consider.

---

* *That said, no long- (or even short-) term studies have been conducted to verify the higher percentage of ill effects attached to the name. I suspect it's just easier to remember the bad things that happen to dogs called Lucky.*

YOU WILL BE USING THE NAME IN PUBLIC.

Although Sweetcheeks might be endearing at home, you run the risk of humiliation—and of having unsavory strangers respond—if you use it when you're shopping with your Maltese in Home Depot.

Be careful, too, of sound-a-likes. My friend Clare had always liked the name Venus, which suggested both strength and beauty—until, that is, she heard it used on the beach. It took a while for her to realize that the dog's owner wasn't attempting to summon a male sex organ.

The converse holds true, too—that is, you might regret choosing a name primarily for its public effect. I'd always wanted to call a dog "Stella"—no matter what the gender—so I could bellow down the street à la Stanley Kowalski. Never mind that I'm not generally a bellower and that not everyone has seen *A Streetcar Named Desire*. I was convinced it would be an endless source of amusement for me and everyone I encountered.

Luckily, I was saved from my worst instincts when the dog I adopted was prenamed Frankie, after the golf partner of his rescuer's husband. Frankie's not a duffer-type pup—although he has been known to pee on the greens at resort courses—but the name nevertheless suited the little guy to a tee.

IRONY GETS OLD QUICKLY.

Lots of people think it's funny to call their Chihuahuas "Tiger" or their Great Danes "Tiny." One man I pass while walking Frankie always says "Hi, Killer" to my shy, pint-sized guy. I was amused maybe the first 10 times he did it, not so much after that.

POP CULTURE REFERENCES ALSO GET DATED, FAST.

Except in the case of Elvis. I personally know two canine Elvises (Elvi?) whose owners are generations apart.

A NAME SHOULDN'T BE TOO LONG OR COMPLEX.

Dogs have fairly short attention spans when it comes to language (as opposed, again, to food; you'll discover that your dog's gaze might remain fixed on your plate for the entire duration of your dinner). By the time you're done saying "Titus Andronicus" or "Princess Grace," your dog will have stopped looking at you and returned to licking his or her privates. One or two syllables—anything you can shout quickly in an emergency—should suffice.

A NAME SHOULD NOT SOUND TOO SIMILAR TO A COMMAND.

If you name a dog Don, for example, he will either spend a lot of time in a down stay position or look at you quizzically whenever you try to put him in one.

A NAME SHOULD NOT SOUND TOO MUCH LIKE THAT OF A NONCANINE MEMBER OF YOUR FAMILY.

Unless, of course, you discover that the similarity helps resolve a child's discipline issues.

A NAME SHOULDN'T BE CHOSEN AS A TRIBUTE TO SOMEONE WHO'S STILL ALIVE.

What might seem like a good idea in puppyhood can turn dicey if the dog becomes fat and flatulent. It's also a good idea to steer clear of the recently departed, lest relatives feel their kin has been disrespected.

Finally, keep in mind that your dog's primary name merely serves as a base for the riffs you'll play on it. Frankie soon became Frankie Doodle because I thought he was dandy.

This morphed into Frankie Doodle, my tiny Poodle, and from that into Poodle Boy. He is also Frankfurter or, if he's being imperious, His Frankiness. Sometimes I call him bat boy because his ears seem capable of echolocation, or honey bunny because he's small and fuzzy … You get the picture.

He doesn't answer to most of these names, of course, but at least I found a way to amuse myself that doesn't involve bellowing "STEH-LUH" down the street.

20. HOW SHOULD I REFER TO MY RELATIONSHIP WITH MY DOG?

I'm afraid this issue is as complicated—and as emotionally fraught—as discussing human partnerships that fall outside the bounds of traditional marriage. The awkward "significant other" is elegant compared to what's involved in describing the human-canine bond.

The term "owner" has become problematic because it implies that a dog is merely property; the more acceptable usage is "guardian" of a "companion animal" (formerly known as a "pet"). The thinking behind movements such as the "Guardian Campaign," being conducted by the California-based In Defense of Animals, is that changing the way we speak about animals changes the way we act towards them. By replacing "ownership," which suggests unbridled power, with "guardianship," which suggests protection, we head off animal abuse, the theory goes.

Hmmm.

Of course Frankie is my companion and I'm constantly reminded that he's an animal, but guardian doesn't come close to describing my indentured servitude to him. When, in return for room, board, medical care, transportation, and poop scooping, Frankie starts pulling his weight by doing the laundry and contributing to the utility bills, I'll consider redefining our relationship. In the meantime, I own his cute little butt.

Perhaps more to the point, "companion" and "guardian" are cold in comparison with the terms of endearment you'll encounter everywhere pet lovers gather, including online. Dogs are regularly referred to as "fur people" or "fur babies," their owners as "moms" and "dads." Me, I'm a bit creeped out by the parenting metaphors. As much as I adore Frankie, I find the notion of having given birth to him or any member of another species rather freakish. And I don't even want to contemplate who the father of such a union might have been—and what unnatural acts I would have had to perform with him. I've therefore decided to start calling Frankie my SCO: Significant Canine Other. This term can be adapted to multidog households, with SCO1, SCO2, and so on used to refer to the order of acquisition (um, assumption of the guardianship role).

21. WHERE SHOULD MY DOG SLEEP?

Wolf-canine analogies loom large in expert opinions on this topic. Dubious as many such comparisons may be, in this case they lead to advice that strikes me as reasonable. To wit, whatever you ultimately decide about sharing your Posture-pedic, it's a good idea to let your new dog stay in the wolf den (a.k.a. your bedroom) initially, to allow her to feel like part of the pack (a.k.a. you and your family). Proximity to your scent is all that's required, so it's fine for her to sleep in her own bed or in a crate. Your dog will never tell you if you're too close, so just choose a place where you won't trip over her if you get up in the middle of the night.

In fact, it's not only fine to keep your dog at a distance at first, but desirable. Because Frankie was so standoffish initially, I was thrilled when he finally deigned to get off the couch and bond with my pillow. But we're talking about a diminutive pup. You might, with good reason, have reservations about letting an 80-pound lug hog the blankets. So play hard to get for a while, at least until you're sure whether or not your dog snores. It's the same as with humans: after you let them into your bed, you have a tough time getting them out.

22. WHAT COMMUNICATION BASICS DO I NEED TO KNOW TO GET OFF ON THE RIGHT FOOT/ PAWS?

Chapter 6 focuses on training in more detail, but some things are useful to keep in mind from the beginning.

DECIDE WHAT YOU WANT FROM YOUR DOG, AND BE CONSISTENT ABOUT ASKING FOR IT

Some people don't mind if their dog shares the sofa with them; others prefer to keep their furniture pup-free. Make up your mind about what you'd like and stick to it; otherwise you'll just confuse your dog.

But don't be inflexible. Your dog may not be capable of conforming to your every lifestyle desire, especially early on. Just establish general principles and work towards them as best you can.

DON'T REWARD FOR BAD BEHAVIOR, AND DON'T SCOLD FOR GOOD

This corollary to the first dictate may seem obvious, but it's surprisingly easy to do the opposite of what you intend. For example, it may initially tickle you to catch your dog nabbing food from the kitchen counter, but if you laugh instead of commanding "No" and distracting your dog the first few times, you're likely to create an unregenerate counter surfer—or at the least one who's baffled by your inconsistency.

Conversely, if you catch your pup behaving badly and call him over to you, don't reprimand him if he responds. He won't associate the tongue-lashing with the act you've interrupted; the only thing you'll have taught him is to avoid coming when summoned.

DON'T TAKE YOUR DOG'S BEHAVIOR PERSONALLY

Dogs will be dogs. They dig, sniff, chew, bark, chase things, fight, and partake in other activities that might render them less-than-perfect housemates, but they don't do it to offend you. So don't take offense—take training classes. And remember, *you* do things that are considered hostile in the dog universe, such as making direct eye contact and giving head pats. Your excuse is no different from theirs: you don't know any better.

AVOID PUP PSYCHOLOGY

Dogs unquestionably have emotions and goals such as achieving pleasure and avoiding pain. But their emotions and goals are not precisely the same as ours. For example, when you come home to discover that your dog has pooped on the rug, don't interpret the expression on her face when she greets you as guilt. It is far more likely to be confusion about why you've suddenly begun barking at her. And pushing her face into the offending (to you) feces will merely indicate that you have some peculiar feeding habits. She would much prefer you to push her face into hamburger and skip the irritating vocal accompaniments.

23. SHOULD I GET MY DOG MICROCHIPPED?

Only if you want to find her if she's lost or stolen.

I bring this topic up now because some dogs make their most dramatic escape attempts before they're fully settled into their new homes.

Yes, a collar with full ID tags is the first line of defense for locating a hound with Houdini tendencies, but it's far easier to ditch a collar than it is to remove an implanted chip. Tattooing, a common identification method in the past, is painful for the dog (who doesn't even get to choose a personalized design); moreover, because they're out of fashion, tattoos are easily overlooked, especially in long-haired breeds.

Not to be confused with a Global Positioning System, a microchip doesn't allow you to locate a lost dog yourself; it's activated by a scanner that's available at most shelters and veterinarian offices—the places to which canine escapees are most likely to be brought. GPSs are good supplements in some cases, but they're expensive, heavier than is comfortable for many small dogs, and only useful if your dog doesn't wiggle out of her collar or a thief doesn't remove it.

Getting a microchip implanted is as quick and easy as a vaccination, and far longer lasting; you almost never have to replace a chip during the dog's lifetime (it's extremely rare for it to migrate from the scruff, where it's placed). And these tiny devices serve not only to identify* your pup when she's turned into the pound, but the databases with which they're affiliated store information about any medical conditions she may have.

Many shelters microchip dogs for free or for a nominal fee; at a vet's office, expect to pay less than $100. The only thing you need to do is register the chip online (generally, at a cost of less than $20) and update the information if you move or change your telephone number. When I couldn't read the numbers on Frankie's ID tag, I was amazed to discover that the act of calling the microchip company from my home phone allowed all his data to be retrieved.

Which leads to an objection some conspiracy theorists have: that it's a slippery slope from microchipping your dog to government-enforced human microchipping. Please. Anyone who goes online, drives past a traffic camera, or enters a convenience store has relinquished all claims to privacy. At least microchipping your dog increases the odds that you'll continue to have warm and friendly companionship in a cold, surveillance-crazy world.

Nor is there any convincing evidence that microchips cause cancer. The odds of harm coming to your dog because he's lost and can't be identified are immeasurably greater than the chance that he'll develop a tumor on the chip site.

---

* One complication: Different microchips are manufactured with different frequencies, from 125 (most common in the United States) to 134.2 kiloherz (used abroad), and not all scanners can read their competitor's chips. But almost all shelters have the ability to read most common microchips—and the method is so useful that it's just a question of time before a universal scanner is perfected and becomes standard equipment.

CHAPTER 3
HEALTH CARE 101

24. HOW DO I FIND A GOOD VETERINARIAN?

Time was when a dog would have a vet for life, a family practitioner for the furry. Veterinary monogamy is no longer a given. Specialization and the explosion of the industry have made pet care very competitive. So take your time, and don't worry if you don't find *"the one"* right away.

Among the many reasons to get a dog from a shelter* or a reputable breeder is that they've vetted many vets and have a good basis for recommendations. Ask dog-connected friends, relatives, and co-workers for referrals, too. Groomers, trainers, and pet boutique proprietors may offer leads, but beware canine cronyism ("I carry your brochure and you carry mine").

Some objective criteria to consider include affiliation with the American Animal Hospital Association (AAHA; www.healthypet.com), which ensures that a facility offers a wide array of equipment and services. It doesn't, however, allow you to evaluate the skill—or the warmth—of each participating doctor. Similarly, membership in a state veterinary association (click on the state resources section of the American Veterinary Medical Association website, www.avma.org) suggests a practitioner's interest in continuing education and animal welfare issues, but not necessarily her ability to relate to patients.

In any case, you're the only one who can judge what's most important to you, including convenience, cost, and approach (for example, openness to alternative medicine). You may not even be aware of your priorities until you visit a vet a few times.

Consider these basics when choosing a practice.

---

* *The only downside: One of the main jobs of vets who volunteer at shelters is neutering/spaying. I attribute Frankie's resistance to the office of the (extremely nice) vet recommended by his rescuer to the fact that he lost his manhood there.*

APPEARANCE

Of the offices, not of the participating vets (although hot-ness is a bonus in any professional you're likely to be seeing on a regular basis). The waiting room should be clean but not sterile, with comfortable chairs and a good use of space, including enough room to keep the nervous dogs from being intimidated by the bullies. The back areas where overnight patients stay and lab work is conducted should be spotless— ditto the vet techs—and the cages should be spacious. And yes, any reputable vet should allow you to tour this back area on the spur of the moment, i.e., without having to yell, "Heads up, pet owner incoming."

BASIC EQUIPMENT

Again, of the office, not the vets. Things such as onsite x-ray equipment, laboratory, and pharmacy mean your dog can get diagnosed and treated expeditiously, and you don't have to run around or phone a lot of different facilities.

NUMBER AND QUALITY OF PARTICIPATING VETS

If you have an emergency and your "primary" isn't available, it's comforting to know that other trustworthy docs have immediate access to your dog's records. You don't have to like the other vets as much as you do your own, but it's desir-able for you to consider them competent. Ideally, a practice should be diverse, including a fresh-out-of-school newbie versed in the latest equipment and techniques as well as a senior person with lots of surgical experience. If there's a clinic in your city affiliated with a university department of veterinary science or college of veterinary medicine, you've hit the jackpot.

COST

The fees for basic procedures such as exams and vaccinations should be in the same ballpark as those of other vets in your town; phone around and ask. Don't consider a practice that makes you feel guilty or cheap for inquiring; it'll only get worse down the road if you're faced with deciding whether you can afford an expensive life-saving procedure (but see question 28). Nix any vet who tries to minimize your financial concerns.

Be suspicious of cutesy names like Paws or The Pet Center. They tend to signify either superficial glitz—soft music, Earth tones, the latest issues of *Dog Fancy* instead of three-year-old copies of the *Economist,* all which will cost you—or bare bones facilities that need a gimmick to draw patients in.

STAFF

Quantity—enough people in the office to ensure efficiency in a large practice—and quality are both important. Staff members should be able to answer basic questions about medical procedures as well as about payment plans, and they should be welcoming to canine patients, no matter how smelly and drooly. If your dog isn't as cute as, say, my Frankie, the receptionist should at least comment on her sweetness, perhaps, or his friendliness. *Note:* The flattery requirement is waived for dogs who make the staff cower behind their desks.

Things to look for in a vet include the following traits.

ACCREDITATION

While your dog is being weighed, take a peek at the diploma on the wall. You want someone with at least a DVM (Doctor of Veterinary Medicine) or equivalent degree (for example, a BVMS or Bachelor of Veterinary Medicine and Surgery, offered in the United Kingdom), preferably from a country you've heard of where they don't eat small domestic animals.

DOGSIDE MANNER

Not all vets are equally kind to their pet patients; I've encountered some who are downright brusque. No pup likes to be probed and prodded but the best vets are skilled in minimizing doggie discomfort with gentle handling, soothing tones—and a well-paced plying of treats. (People doctors should consider adopting this last technique; I'd bet a few Godiva chocolates would go a long way toward mitigating the stress of a gynecological exam.)

PEOPLE SKILLS

Sure, the vet's attitude toward your dog is foremost, but you need to be able to provide follow-up care, so instructions need to be clear. And there's no excuse for a vet to be patronizing; remember, a good part of her day is spent inserting thermometers into small animal butts. Finally, as with the members of his staff, a vet should say flattering things about your dog—or at least should avoid insults. One vet told me that Frankie was "weird" and a "bad patient" because he wouldn't pee for the techs who walked him during an all-day diagnostic stay. Frankie is an extremely skilled urinater when he so desires, thank you very much, but he's not a pee-on-demand pup.

25. HOW SOON DO I NEED TO BRING MY DOG TO THE VET?

Very soon. If you get a dog who hasn't had a verified health exam or thorough temperament evaluation, don't even take her home; head straight for the vet. Sad but true: If something is seriously wrong you need to know before you bond with the pup and spend vast quantities of money and emotional energy on her.

If you get a dog with a clean preliminary bill of health, see the vet within the first few weeks of her homecoming. Puppies need a series of vaccinations (see question 30) and healthy older dogs need a "wellness" exam to serve as a baseline for future diagnoses. You'll also want to get some guidelines for what's normal—in addition to those sketched in question 33 —as soon as possible.

26. HOW CAN I MAKE THE MOST OUT OF A VET VISIT?

By observing a few basic rules of vet-iquette.

GET A NEW ATTITUDE

Avoid sending stress signals to your dog about an upcoming visit. Puppies don't have any negative preconceptions about doctors, and an adult dog who's new to you might pick up on your positive cues. Try pretending that you're going to a sedate dog park where pups and their people get to spend some quiet quality time together.

BE NICE TO THE SUPPORT STAFF

They're the ones who put you on hold—or not—when you phone, put the messages on the vet's desk—or not—and generally oil the office wheels. Just as staff members need to say nice things about your dog, you in turn are well advised to compliment staff hairstyles, jewelry, virility—whatever works.

BE ON YOUR BEST BEHAVIOR

By which I mean, make sure your dog is on his. He may not be fully trained yet but, in the case of a large dog, work on "sit" and "down" commands before you come in, the better to avoid disturbing other patients and their accompanying people. Small pups should be kept in your lap if they're excitable; it's also a good way to keep them from picking up germs from the floor.

BRING ALONG A LIST OF QUESTIONS

Especially early on, you'll have plenty of things to ask about what to expect. Try to remember to commit these questions to paper—and to take the paper along with you.

TELL THE TRUTH, NO MATTER HOW EMBARRASSING

If you bring your dog in with stomach distress, don't pretend you didn't see him scarfing down the discarded condoms near your bed. You don't have to say what you were doing—or with whom—while those condoms were being consumed, or even what size they were. Sure, your vet might laugh about it at the bar with his friends later but at least your dog will get the correct treatment.

EXPRESS YOURSELF

Although it's the vet's responsibility to try to be clear, she's not a mind reader, so follow up on anything you don't understand. And voice your concerns, no matter how peculiar (poop eating) or petty (nail clipping) they may seem. As it happens, feces feasting is not all that uncommon, and clipping a dog's nails may help prevent painful infections.

DON'T SECOND-GUESS YOUR VET

Reading up on medical issues on the Internet or elsewhere has its limits. It's good to be an informed consumer, the better to ask educated questions, but not useful to argue when your vet expresses an opinion that's based on education and experience—and thus a far greater ability to interpret data. And remember that your vet is looking at your actual dog, not a theoretical on-line case. If you have serious doubts about a diagnosis, it's fine to inquire how the vet arrived at it or ask for clarification. Just don't start your sentence with, "But I read on the Internet...." It's perfectly fine, on the other hand, to ask your vet if she can recommend some helpful websites.

TAKE NOTES—AND MAKE A PLAN

Dogs are notoriously bad at remembering details and even worse at writing things down; you'll be expected to do both if you want to remember what was said during the exam. Perhaps one of the most important things to jot down is the blueprint for what comes next: "So we come back in six months for a follow-up exam?" Or, "I'll make an appointment for a teeth cleaning as soon as that gum infection is cleared up?"

27. SHOULD I GET HEALTH INSURANCE FOR MY DOG?

Hell, yes—and the sooner the better. The younger and the healthier your dog, the more insurable she will be and the lower the premiums you'll pay. Pet insurance isn't yet as popular as it's bound to become, which is why it didn't occur to me to get it. Now I kick myself for not having thought to insure Frankie, who, without any predictors, developed diabetes. This chronic, preexisting condition pretty much eliminates my sugar-sweet pup from the pool of insurable pooches. And I can't even claim him as a dependent on my tax returns.

Yes, insurance is an additional monthly expense, but it's an anticipated one that you can budget for. Premiums are fairly reasonable and not having to factor in cost when facing the decision of whether to provide treatment—priceless. Why join the ranks of the estimated 73 percent of people willing to go into debt for their pets?

Another reason to get in on pet insurance now: because it's set up so that you pay for treatment up front and fill out the forms for reimbursement, vets don't have to deal with a bureaucracy. And pet insurance companies don't dictate conventional treatment choices—yet.

That's not to say you don't have to do research to get the best deal. Things to consider for comprehensive insurance plans—which are different from discount plans where you pay an annual fee in return for lower prices on vet services—are similar to what you'd look for in human plans. Just be sure to read the fine print. In some cases, for example, claims have to be submitted within 60 days to be accepted.

Take the following items into account when deciding on pet health insurance.

CHOICE OF VETERINARIAN

Most plans let you see anyone you like; others are similar to HMOs, limiting you to certain health-care providers.

WAITING PERIOD

There's usually at least a 10-day wait so that people don't sign up immediately after their dog leaps off a precipice. Check and see when a policy will take effect—and watch your pup like a hawk until then.

RATE GUARANTEE

Some companies adjust their premiums on a quarterly basis; that means if they pay a claim they can raise your rates in the next period. Make sure the company you choose offers contracts for at least one year, with no fee-rise adjustments if you submit a claim.

RENEWABILITY

You want a plan that doesn't consider a condition diagnosed after you first contracted with the company as preexisting, and thus as a reason for not renewing your insurance.

EXCLUSIONS

Typically, dogs younger than six to eight weeks and those older than eight to ten years are ineligible for insurance. Those with preexisting conditions and breed-specific heredi-tary conditions are generally excluded, too, though in some cases you can pay extra for coverage. Another reason to get a mutt: they're more easily insured.

WELLNESS

Things like dental care, vaccinations, and heartworm testing should be covered. Some plans don't take care of neutering or spaying, but that shouldn't be a deal breaker as clinics often offer deep discounts for those procedures.

PRESCRIPTIONS

You often end up spending far more money on medicines than on office visits and services, so be sure your plan offers good coverage.

DEDUCTIBLES

As with human plans, the higher the deductible, the lower your premium.

SPECIFICITY

You'll find plans that say they reimburse you for "reasonable and customary fees." That's way too much wiggle room. You're far better off with an insurer that provides a chart detailing what you can expect to get back for what you pay out.

CAPS

There's usually an annual limit for what a company will reimburse. Find out if there's also a limit to what insurance will pay for a specific incident.

Although you still have fewer choices for pet insurance than for auto or homeowners' insurance, more and more companies are entering the field every month. Those with proven track records include Veterinary Pet Insurance (www.petinsurance. com) and PetCare (www.petcareinsurance.com). Both the ASPCA (www.aspcapetinsurance.com) and the AKC (www. akcphp.com/BHIACMS/) have recently introduced policies, and the Humane Society features discounts on PetPlan (www.gopetplan.com). Check www.PetInsuranceReview.com to get real people feedback on some of the most widely used plans.

28. IS THERE SUCH A THING AS ALTERNATIVE MEDICINE FOR DOGS?

Naturally. The American Holistic Veterinary Medical Association (ahvma.org; log on to find practitioners in your area) dates back to 1982, and the popularity of its doggie "modalities," including acupuncture, homeopathy, herbal medicine, and chiropractic, parallels that of its human counterparts. The monthly *Whole Dog Journal* (www.whole-dog-journal. com) details the latest in natural dog care, while *Natural Remedies Dogs and Cats Wish You Knew* by Viv Harris outlines treatments for problems ranging from allergies to cancer.

I'm no slave to conventional medicine but my forays into the alternative arena haven't been terribly successful. Most recently, the search for a nutritionist to help with Frankie's diabetes led us to Dr. B., who determined that Frankie's neutering scar was blocking the blood flow to his pancreas. Her suggested remedy: rub flaxseed oil into the area. Initially blissed out by these ministrations—his testicles might be MIA, but his penis hasn't left the neighborhood—Frankie soon began to squirm away in shame. I immediately ceased treatment. Nevertheless, on our next visit Dr. B. judged the blockage cleared and praised my persistence. I went back to my traditional vet, and Frankie and I resumed our previous, more decorous relationship.

So do what you think works for you and your dog—but not on your own. Take the "complementary" and "integrative" claims of alternative practices seriously: make sure they complement and integrate with the advice of a person who has completed at least four years of veterinary school. The same goes for supplements; just because something's labeled "natural" doesn't mean that it's not naturally toxic to your dog, or that it's not contraindicated with another supplement or medication she's taking.

29. HOW WILL NEUTERING OR SPAYING AFFECT MY DOG?

Perhaps a more relevant question is how will it affect *you*? There's no evidence that "fixing" causes adverse medical reactions; quite the opposite, in fact. The notion that altering interferes with the development of certain breeds' distinctive look has been debunked, too. Instead, it's been shown that the accompanying growth slowdown allows joints and bones to develop correctly. Dogs that have been neutered or spayed tend to grow larger than their unfixed littermates, too. Moreover, dogs don't have ego issues connected with their sex organs, nor do they sentimentalize motherhood. So if you're not a breeder, any reservations about having your dog's uterus or testicles removed are pure projection. (Admit it, the anatomical precision of that description made you more uncomfortable than the terms spaying or neutering. Your dog, on the other hand, would react equally—i.e., not at all—to either expression.)

A prime reason to spay or neuter your dog is to be a good global citizen. One busy bitch can produce as many as 67,000 descendants, exponentially, in six years, and some six to eight million dogs and cats are euthanized annually in the United States alone. Dogs don't have impulse control and they don't practice safe sex, so it's up to you to ensure that they don't contribute to the misery of their species.

But spaying and neutering offer less altruistic benefits. A female who's been spayed won't go into heat, as her twice-yearly reproductive cycles are called—which means less mess for you, less discomfort for her (although as far as I know, no studies have been done about doggie menstrual cramps and PMS), and less upheaval for everyone because hordes of panting male suitors won't be coming to call. Spayed females also run a lower risk of mammary gland (breast) cancer—not to mention zero risk of uterine and ovarian cancer.

For males, early neutering can minimize aggression; roaming (guy pups are literally heat-seeking missiles, always on the prowl for those busy bitches); and, in some cases, marking (thus allowing you to take a walk without stopping every two seconds for pee dispersal). Neutering may also keep males from humping inappropriate love objects like the legs of your houseguests. Without the distraction of raging hormones, they're also better able to concentrate on training. Naturally, neutering also eliminates the possibility of testicular cancer.

Those who have a problem with unmanning—undogging?—their pooches can pretend it didn't happen by investing in Neuticles (www.neuticles.com).* Allowing your dog "to retain his natural look" and "self-esteem," these silicon nut substitutes are available in three sizes and three degrees of

---

* The "testicular prosthetic implants"—used by nearly a quarter million pet owners, according to the website—earned their creator, Gregg A. Miller, the IG Nobel Prize for Medicine in 2005. Upon receiving the oddly coveted spoof award from Harvard University's Annals of Improbable Research, Miller said in a videotaped statement, "Considering my parents thought I was an idiot when I was a kid, this is a great honor."

firmness. Prices range from $109 per pair for the original rigid ones for small dogs to $1,799 for a customized set of the more pliant ones. I shudder to think how many dog balls needed to be handled to perfect this invention.

The jury is still out on the best age for spaying and neutering. Conventional wisdom once had it that females should be allowed to go through one heat cycle before surgery, but that's no longer advised (presumably to the dismay of the manufacturers of Bitch Britches, also called season panties). The suggested spaying age is now five to six months, preceding the first heat. Similarly, where four to six months used to be the recommended age for neutering, some vets now say that males as young as eight weeks can safely undergo the operation (though you'd have to wait a while to insert adult-size Neuticles). Although vet consensus is that it's best to neuter early, before the behaviors the procedure are meant to prevent become ingrained, most agree that neutering can be useful in diminishing aggression later in life, too. Apparently, testosterone poisoning isn't limited to the very young.

30. WHAT'S THE LATEST WORD ON VACCINATIONS?

Individualize. There's no question that vaccinations are essential to your dog's health, but views on the efficacy, frequency, risk, and even type of shots required have shifted in recent years. Annual boosters are no longer advised for most vaccines, for example; three-year updates are now considered sufficient. Similarly, because research has shown that not all vaccines remain effective for the same length of time, the practice of bundling—putting several vaccines together in a single shot—is becoming less common.* In short, a

---

* Unfortunately, state laws and drug manufacturers don't always keep up with medical science. Some states require annual rabies shots, even though professionals agree they're only needed every three years. And some manufacturers haven't changed the frequency instructions on their vaccines. This puts vets into the uncomfortable position of having to ignore product recommendations—or risk harming their patients.

no-shot-fits-all philosophy is emerging. A responsible vet
should take the age, breed, habits, and immune system of
your dog—as well as the region in which you live—into
account when determining which inoculations to give.

Vaccines fall into two basic categories: the core group, which
protect against diseases that are particularly dangerous, are
easily transmitted, and/or are dangerous to humans, including distemper, adenovirus, parvovirus, and rabies; and the
noncore group, recommended for dogs at specific risk.
Desert-dwelling dogs don't have to worry about Lyme disease,
for example, as those who live in humid, tick-rich areas do;
and pups who don't go to doggie daycare or engage in group
overnight sleepaways need not be inoculated against kennel
cough. Even with core group medications, however, vaccinations should be considered on an individual basis. The risks
of vaccinating very old dogs, dogs with compromised immune systems, and certain toy breeds, say, may outweigh the
benefits.

Lately, there's been a good deal of interest in titer tests,
which determine the continuing effectiveness of a vaccine
by measuring the level of antibodies present in the blood. At
this point, however, many of these tests aren't considered

accurate enough to justify their expense. Results are not consistent for all diseases—many researchers consider only those for distemper and parvo reliable—or even for all breeds.

The bottom line: A series of core group shots are recommended for puppies as soon as they've lost their mothers' immunity, at around four weeks; at the latest, these initial shots should be given at six months. After two years of age, tread—or shoot—lightly. Don't second guess your vet, but stay informed.

31. AT WHAT AGE SHOULD I GET MY DOG'S EARS CROPPED AND TAIL DOCKED?

At no age, if most veterinarians have their say. Cropping and docking have been outlawed in many countries, and the American Veterinary Medical Association's policy statement dubs these surgeries "not medically indicated, nor of benefit to the patient," noting that they "cause pain and distress."

Historically, tail docking, or surgical shortening, helped prevent working dogs from getting injured. For example, overlong tails of hunting dogs running through brush to retrieve prey might get burrs caught in them, and sheepdogs might be mistaken for wolves threatening the herds and get shot in error. Cutting and bandaging a dog's ears to make them stand upright, on the other hand, was always purely aesthetic, done to make guard dogs like Boxers and Dobermans look fierce and alert. Now most of these cosmetic procedures are performed—usually without anesthesia in early puppyhood—to make dogs conform to the American Kennel Club's breed registry standards.

In addition to being cruel and—except in working dogs—useless, tail docking also interferes with communication. How can you know what your dog is trying to tell you if he doesn't have a tail? And I think cropped ears make a pup appear not so much fierce as astonished—the same look you get from a too-tight facelift.

32. WHAT'S THE BEST WAY TO KEEP MY DOG HEALTHY?

Dogs need to do the same things that we need to do to stay in shape: eat well and get plenty of exercise. Luckily, it's an easier regimen to enforce than to stick to: your dog can't binge on junk food unless you provide it (or he lucks into a McDonald's dumpster), and you'll never hear him complain, "Sorry, I'm just not up for walking today."*

When it comes to disease, human-canine principles converge, too, with prevention, early detection, and early correction being key.

PREVENTION

To keep your dog from getting seriously ill you need to ...

- 🦴 Vaccinate (see question 30)
- 🦴 De-bug
- 🦴 Brush teeth

Parasites such as heartworm, fleas, ticks, and mosquitoes are more than just nuisances to dogs; they can be deadly. Pet store shelves are filled with products to eliminate them: pills, topical creams, single doses, combinations ... But don't use anything without consulting your vet.** If your dog already has heartworm, for example, and you give him preventative

---

* Unless it's raining, in which case all bets are off.

** Except for the natural sprays that keep pests away from your dog. Some flea and tick medications have turned out to be toxic to dogs as well as to the critters they're hosting. I'm all for avoiding harsh chemicals whenever possible, just not for ingesting unknown botanicals in lieu of medicine.

medication for it, the nuked worms can clog his cardio-vascular system (how's that for a scare tactic?). And cat medications—even if they look the same as dog remedies and are on sale—can make your dog sick. What part of "different species" don't you understand?

Yes, you need to brush your dog's teeth. I'll explain why in Chapter 4.

EARLY DETECTION

Early detection is important in maintaining your dog's health.

BE HANDS ON—LITERALLY

One of the advantages of brushing your dog's coat regularly is that you can feel for any new growths or scabs. While you've got him in that pleasure zone of grooming, peer into and sniff at his ears (there's more on all this in Chapter 5).

Be observant

A change in habits—especially drinking, eating, and elimination—can presage illness.

See your vet annually

Take your dog for a yearly vet visit (twice a year for a senior pet), even if your dog seems fine.

Early correction

Don't procrastinate. If you don't take care of a health problem as soon as you discover it, it can get out of hand—and thus become even more expensive to deal with than it was initially.

33. HOW DO I KNOW WHAT'S NORMAL VERSUS WHAT I NEED TO WORRY ABOUT?

Dogs do a lot of stuff that seems very strange to us and perplexes even people with advanced degrees in animalology. Because it's comforting to know what behavior belongs in the realm of peculiar but not unique, here are some of the most common examples of the peculiar.

EATING

Some dogs eat dirt and/or grass. Others down nonorganic foreign objects, like TV remotes and pantyhose. And still others eat feces—their own, other dogs', other species'. (There's even a term for this taste for waste—coprophagia.)

No one is entirely sure why dogs have such eclectic palates. The consumption of indigestible items is the biggest problem, because you'll have to pay for surgery if those pantyhose don't pass through without incident. But it's the poop-eating that seems to drive people craziest, even though it's not generally harmful. My dog's adorable, they protest. How could he be so disgusting? Proposed cures include putting meat tenderizer in your dog's food—apparently it makes the poop less yummy—or sprinkling Bitter Apple on the turds. The most logical solution: clean up after your dog immediately.*

BREATHING/VOCALIZATIONS

Along with barking and howling, dogs pant. It's their method of air-conditioning: they cool themselves off by increasing evaporation in the respiratory tract. Some dogs don't pant much, except when it's really warm or after strenuous exercise. Others pant at the drop of a hat, whenever they're excited or nervous. The length of panting varies, too. The particular

---

* *Keeping your dog out of kitty litter could be more complicated, because it's not right to make the cat climb to a place that's inaccessible to the dog to go to the bathroom. I suggest you find the cat another home.*

functioning of your dog's self-cooling unit will soon become evident to you.

Dogs also produce many un-doglike vocalizations. When I first heard Frankie sigh, for example, I was terrified that he was the reincarnation of my mother, queen of the emotionally fraught exhalation. I've come to see that, although Frankie inspires guilt in his own special way, his sighs signal impatience or satisfaction rather than disappointment with me. At least that's what I've chosen to convince myself they mean.

ELIMINATING

Watch for differences when your dog goes to the bathroom.

Liquid

Marking is the stop-and-start, back-leg-raised urinating that unneutered males do to say "I was here" (also known as pee-mail) or "I see your pee and I pee on it!" (a form of pooch poker called four-legged stud). But cross-peeing is also quite common: some laid-back males, even those neutered late, squat and empty their bladders completely, while some alpha females raise their legs and pee in short bursts. So don't worry if your pup likes to urinate outside gender stereotypes.

Solid

I've already discussed feces eating. Dogs also do something called "scooting" or "scooching": dragging their behinds across the grass, the floor, or—particularly popular—your white rug. This might indicate something as simple as that your dog's butt itches or that she wants to dislodge some dingleberries; it might, on the other hand, indicate that her anal "glands"—the small, scent-bearing sacs that inspire dogs to sniff each other's butts—need to be drained.

Some people perform the fairly simple procedure of squeezing (expressing) these sacs at home, after being instructed on how to do so by a vet. Others—and I include myself in this category—are completely grossed out by the idea. What smells good to a dog doesn't always synch with human olfactory preferences, especially in concentrated form. I therefore pay a groomer to do it.

MOVING

Digging comes naturally to many dogs, particularly terriers and other working breeds taught to keep their hunters' prey protected underground. These Earth relocation projects don't have to have an object; some dogs simply like digging for its own sake. Some digging, however, is related to burying food, toys, or anything else your dog wants to save for later. I wouldn't worry about hoarding unless your dog takes his kibble, bit by bit, to the backyard.

Perhaps more disconcerting than digging is the circling and scratching that many dogs do before they lie down. Some hypothesize that this might be a vestige from the days when wolves needed to clear snakes or other pests from the den. Sometimes Frankie roots around vigorously before he goes to sleep; sometimes he doesn't bother. I've never tried to determine whether there's a correlation between the length of his exploratory gestures and the cleanliness of my sheets.

And yes, there are doggie shrinks—called behaviorists. I'll talk more about them in Chapter 6.

34. WHAT SHOULD I DO IN CASE OF EMERGENCY?

Be prepared. And try to stay calm.

Keep the number and address of your nearest emergency (24-hour) veterinary facility and the ASPCA's poison control hotline (1-888-426-4435) on your refrigerator and in your wallet. Keep a credit card number handy, too; there's a $60 fee for the poison hotline, and you'll be expected to pay a deposit for emergency care. Also, have a couple of people lined up who'll be able to help you get to the vet while you tend to your dog if necessary.

Put together or buy a first-aid kit (they're available at mega pet stores or large discount retailers). It should include the following:

- Muzzle, or the materials to improvise one (including a belt or necktie)

- Sterile gauze pads and gauze bandage rolls

- First-aid adhesive tape

- Nonstick bandages

- Tweezers

- Scissors

- Resealable plastic bags

- Three percent hydrogen peroxide

- Antibacterial ointment

- Eyedropper

- Milk of Magnesia or activated charcoal

- Digital or rectal thermometer

- Splint materials (tongue depressor or 12-inch wooden ruler)

Have protective leather gloves, clean towels, and a blanket on hand, too.

Before trying to examine your dog so you can describe her symptoms to the emergency vet, muzzle her.* When in pain, your ordinarily laid-back pup might lash out with her teeth. You won't be much help to her if you require medical assistance yourself.

First-aid classes and videos, especially those demonstrating CPR, are useful, but—except for keeping your dog still if you fear bone breaks or internal injury or trying to stop profuse bleeding by applying pressure—you should generally avoid doing anything without the advice of the professional whose number you'll have on hand.

One exception: As I've mentioned, dogs eat weird stuff all the time, so it's useful to know that you can perform a doggie Heimlich procedure. Just be sure your dog is actually choking, as opposed to having breathing problems: signs include pawing at the face and throat and attempting to cough, as well as blue lips.

When you're certain your dog's throat is obstructed ...

🦴　Try to calm her; fright might make her try to bite you when you open her mouth.

🦴　Look down her throat to try to find the blockage. Make sure you actually see and identify something rather than just sticking your hand down and tugging at whatever seems not to belong. Dogs have small bones in their necks that can easily be mistaken for a stick or chicken bone.

🦴　Use tweezers (or pliers) to try to remove the object, *carefully*; don't accidentally move the object farther down the throat.

---

* *Do I have to tell you that this doesn't apply if your dog is choking or throwing up?*

🦴   If you can't see or easily get at anything, lift your dog's rear legs or, if she's small enough, hold her upside down by the hips. Gravity is your friend.

🦴   Still nada? With your dog standing, put your hands below her rib cage and pull up into her abdomen quickly five times. If nothing comes out, try looking down her throat again; you may be able to see something now.

I don't recommend doing this in a moving car—especially not one you're driving—but you'll want to get to a vet as soon as possible, even if you manage to get your dog to cough up the goods (or, I should say, the bads).

35. ENOUGH ABOUT MY DOG'S HEALTH. CAN MY DOG MAKE *ME* SICK?

For the most part, no—at least not in the usual sense of transmitting diseases.* Although pups and people suffer from some similar ailments, germs and viruses tend to be species specific. True, bugs and parasites that are dangerous to humans can pass unmolested through canine intestines—but that's only a problem if you pick up dog poop with your bare hands or don't wash up after playing with your dog in the dirt where he's pooped in the past. Somewhat less disgusting but no less lacking in common sense would be removing a disease-bearing tick from your dog without safely disposing of it, thus allowing the little bloodsucker to get under your skin.

And, yes, you can get rabies if your rabid dog bites you, but if you own a vicious dog that hasn't been vaccinated, I somehow doubt you're reading this book.

---

* *Dogs do have bacteria in their gums/teeth that are not good for you, but they're only transmitted if you keep your mouth open when your dog kisses you or if you lick your own face right after your dog does.*

Dog owners are, however, subject to a group of less widely reported and thus more insidious Canine-Related Injuries (CRIs). According to the Centers for Disease Control (CDC), an average of 76,500 people per year trip over their dogs. Most incidents occur during walks, when 31.3 percent reported that they "fell or tripped over the dog" and another 21.2 percent admitted they were "pushed or pulled by the dog." These statistics, based on data from emergency room visits, likely represent only a fraction of actual CRIs because, according to the CDC, "many people don't seek treatment after injuring themselves in accidents involving their pets."

Or they seek treatment outside of emergency rooms. A physical therapist friend told me that she has seen multiple cases of dislocated shoulders caused by sudden and vigorous tugging on the leash. A less typical CRI, but one with which I have personal experience, is tendonitis of the wrist that can result from letting a small dog rest his head on your hand while you're typing.

Most CRIs can be prevented by training—both of you and your dog. Work on ways to get your dog to stop tugging at the leash and to remind yourself to watch for underfoot pups.

More difficult is to train yourself to use common sense—say, when it comes to refusing your pup his chosen headrest.

But the health benefits that dogs confer far outweigh any potential problems. Studies have shown that dogs—and, okay, other warm-blooded pets that shall remain nameless—lower blood pressure and cholesterol; stave off depression; and hasten recovery from major surgery. And that's just for starters. So go kiss your dog, and let her kiss you back. Just don't lick your own face directly afterwards.

CHAPTER 4
CHOWING DOWN

36. HOW MUCH—AND HOW OFTEN—SHOULD I FEED MY DOG?

Not as much—and not as often—as he'd like you to. Dogs have the stockpile-for-starvation gene, which dictates, "Eat! You never know when you'll see your next meal."* So unless you have a very evolved pup, he's not going to stop chowing down just because he's no longer hungry. The amount your dog actually needs—as opposed to what he'll eat—depends on his metabolism, age, and activity level, as well as on the type of food involved.

I once used a dog sitter who didn't grasp this concept. She called me in a panic on the fourth morning of a trip because Frankie was throwing up copiously on every visible surface (but particularly on those that are tough to clean, like the couch and rugs). It turned out that she had ignored my written instructions and served Frankie vast bowls of food, which he happily consumed—until his 11-pound body rebelled. Running mini-marathons might have compensated for his gluttony, but Frankie takes his house-guarding duties very seriously while I'm gone, refusing to venture beyond the backyard. Home protection doesn't burn very many calories.

The dog sitter's defense—that she only fed Frankie the specified two times a day—brings me to the question of frequency. Because of their feast-and-famine pasts, dogs are designed to go without food for long periods. How long a period between feedings you want to enforce will depend on convenience—and guilt. If you're around your dog all day, he will try his best to wheedle food out of you. Twice-daily feedings give you less reason to project, "He must be hungry; I would be." If you're away for a large part of the day—or aren't swayed by pleading looks—then feeding once a day is generally fine. Although dogs don't have a preference, most people, and

---

* This gene also occurs in some human ethnic groups, where it's passed along matrilineally.

especially those who leave home for work, prefer morning feedings, on the premise that a satisfied dog won't feel the need to chew on shoes or furniture (in Chapter 7, I also discuss keeping your dog occupied by putting part of his morning meal in a puzzle toy). And morning feedings eliminate the fear that your dog is only happy to see you when you get home because you're a meal ticket.

For large, deep-chested breeds that are prone to bloat—a life-threatening condition that requires surgery, not just a little gas—feeding smaller portions twice or even three times a day is a better plan. Some people even advocate free-feeding for these breeds, i.e., leaving food around all day so they won't inhale their food at mealtimes. Free-feeding is not recommended in general, however, not only because it's an invitation for most dogs to overeat, but also because constant access to food can make pups finicky.

37. WHAT ABOUT TREATS?

In theory, treats should be reserved as training aids or as pet sitters. That is, foods that take a long time to consume—for example, peanut butter stuffed into a rubber Kong cone—are the canine version of popping your kid in front of a video when you need a bit of quiet time or when you're away from home.

In reality, it's tough to resist a hang-dog look or the urge to reward your pup for sheer doginess. Healthy snacks are a good way to resolve the dilemma. Dog biscuits and other cookielike products with little nutritional value—and huge price markups—are designed to appeal to *you*. Dogs don't associate apple slices, raw carrots, string beans, dried chicken strips, and other pooch-paunch deterrents with deprivation. So don't tell them.

Along with monitoring their nutritional content, you should dole out nontraining treats according to a set routine, the better to prevent free-floating begging. For example, Frankie gets something to nosh on whenever I sit down to eat—which makes me aware just how frequently this occurs. And my best friend Clare gives her dog Archie a snack whenever she opens a bottle of wine. As a friend of hers observed, "When Archie is obese, we'll know you're an alcoholic."*

38. IS IT OKAY TO MAKE MY DOG A VEGETARIAN?

Not really. If you became a vegetarian to avoid cruelty to animals, why practice it on the one you've chosen to share your home with? Your dog could survive on a nonmeat diet, but she wouldn't thrive. That doesn't mean meat has to comprise the bulk of her menu, or that you have to handle uncooked hunks of it; leave the raw food diet (see question 45) to the carnivores.

39. WHAT'S BEST—WET OR DRY FOOD?

It depends on your dog—and on your budget.

Dry food or kibble is generally more economical than wet food and better for dental health because it's abrasive. Kibble is not necessarily as nutritious as wet food, however (which isn't saying much, in many cases of both varieties; see the following question). The canning process allows for the inclusion of a higher percentage of meat and the exclusion of chemical preservatives.

And wet food tends to be more palatable. Many dogs aren't wild about unadorned pellets—would you be?—so lots of

---

* *Because he was originally cued by the sound of the cork being pulled from the bottle, screw tops allowed Clare to sneak tipples—until Archie figured out that he should be on the alert for opening doors of the cabinet where the wine glasses are stored.*

people liven them up with anything from chicken broth to cottage cheese or wet food. This reduces the convenience and economy of kibble.

Smaller dogs and older ones with diminished appetites are often prime candidates for wet food, and big, young lugs usually do fine with kibble. In short, consider such variables as the size, health, and activity level of your dog—and your gag reflex. Dogs often love canned food but they love garbage, too. You may have a tough time dishing out a morning repast that looks and smells repellent to you.

40. WITH SO MANY DIFFERENT TYPES OF KIBBLE AND CANNED FOOD ON THE MARKET, HOW DO I KNOW WHICH TO BUY?

Let's start with what you can ignore when trying to decide about both varieties: terms such as "premium," "gourmet," "natural," "sensible," "scientific," and "holistic" are all meaningless buzz words designed to push your "I'm-a-good-dog-owner" buttons. Don't bother paying attention to the pictures, either; that nice-looking steak on the package or can bears little resemblance to any meat form that might be inside. Nor does the name of the product provide much useful information. Something called "chicken formula" only has to include 25 percent of chicken products—not chicken meat—by weight. "With chicken" means only 3 percent chicken in some variation needs to be present.

For a better sense of what you're buying, go straight to the ingredients list, arranged in order of weight. Even here, you're on shaky ground. The ingredient specifications outlined by the Association of American Feed Control Officials (AAFCO), which regulates the pet food industry, are a canine Da Vinci Code. The "crude protein" requirement, for example, says nothing about digestibility, so the protein source could be old shoes. For additional information—including details on the limitations of AAFCO,* which has close ties to the industry it's designed to police—see The Dog Food Project, www. dogfoodproject.com.

The best practical guides to what to feed your pup are the *Whole Dog Journal*'s (www.whole-dog-journal.com) annual reviews of dry and wet dog foods. These not only explain labels and provide formulas for calculating nutrient levels but also recommend and pan specific products.

So with the caveat that this is just a rough outline, you want a wet or dry food that ...

CONTAINS MORE PROTEIN THAN GRAIN

Having meat or another protein source as the first ingredient should be enough to ensure that the product is indeed primarily protein. But some manufacturers are sneaky, breaking down less desirable ingredients into component parts to get around putting them at the top of the list. For example, they might cite chicken first, followed by ground corn, corn gluten, corn bran—which, in combination, outweigh the chicken.

CONTAINS *IDENDITIFIABLE* PROTEINS AND FATS

The protein source should have a recognizable, not generic, name. That is, it should be "beef," "lamb," "turkey," or "chicken" as opposed to "meat," "animal," or "poultry." That's true too for the "meals"—for example, "chicken meal" as opposed to "poultry meal." Avoid by-products and

---

* *Among these limitations is the fact that, to achieve "nutritional balance," AAFCO regulations stipulate that vitamin and mineral supplements must be added. Because these cannot be organically produced, USDA Organic certification and the AAFCO seal are mutually exclusive. Many vets—including mine—warn patients away from food that isn't AAFCO approved, but I'm no longer convinced of the value of its imprimatur. Put it this way: AAFCO is even less effective (in part because it has even fewer inspectors) and more tainted by agribusiness interests than the FDA is.*

especially unnamed ones, altogether. In spite of their grainy-sounding appellations, meals are not undesirable—under AAFCO definitions, they're required to include meat, skin, and possibly bones in dehydrated form, but *not* feathers, hair, innards, and other, even more disgusting things (appetite spoiler alert: for example, tumors or euthanized dogs).

Fats and oils, essential for skin and coat health, should have specific names, too. So you want "chicken fat" rather than "animal fat," "herring oil" rather than "fish oil," "sunflower oil" rather than "vegetable oil," and so on. Avoid anything that contains mineral oil altogether, because the "mineral" from which it's derived tends to be petroleum.

CONTAINS WHOLE GRAINS OR INTACT CARBOHYDRATE SOURCES

Look for whole grains like brown rice (as opposed to brewer's rice), oatmeal, and whole ground barley, not "fragments" or flour. Corn is not always bad for dogs—though many are sensitive to it—but it has little redeeming nutritional value when in its most common pet food form: as a filler. Similarly, ingredients such as soybean meal, beet pulp, and cereal food, while not necessarily unhealthy on their own in small amounts, are cheap by-products of human food manufacturers that often turn up in pet products produced by the same companies. Sweet potatoes, potatoes, peas, and other starches that tend to turn up in higher-quality dog food are fine as carbohydrates sources.

CONTAINS NATURAL PRESERVATIVES

You'll want derivatives of Vitamin E and C, including the former in its "mixed tocopherols" incarnation, the latter in forms like rosemary-, sage-, and clove extract, ascorbyl palmitate, and ascorbic acid. Avoid the scarier acronyms: BHA, BHT, and TBHQ, along with ethoxyquin and sodium metabisulphite.

DOESN'T CONTAIN FOOD COLORINGS, SWEETENERS, OR SALT

Dogs don't care about the hue of their food, so avoid anything that contains "numbered" dyes such as Red 40; they're designed to make greyish meat products look more genuinely meaty. Caramel coloring is probably the least noxious of these cover-ups.

Dogs do, on the other hand, fall for the unhealthy sweeteners that often turn up in poor-quality food to make them more palatable. They include cane molasses, corn syrup in any form, sugar, sorbitol, sucrose, fructose, glucose, ammoniated glycyrrhizin (the name alone should be enough to warn you off), and propylene glycol.* Blackstrap molasses and honey are fine when consumed sparingly in treats; you just don't want large amounts of them in anything your dog eats on a regular basis, lest your pup start jonesing for sweets.

The same goes for salt (a.k.a. sodium chloride on many packages), which is no better for your dog than it is for you. As with sugar, it's used to make generic meat products more appealing. Give your dog enough food with this needless seasoning and he'll soon be competing with you for the pretzels and popcorn.

41. ARE DRY AND CANNED FOOD THE ONLY OPTIONS?

No. Premixed (but requiring you to add ingredients such as meat and water), freeze-dried, dehydrated, rolled, frozen, and fresh-chilled (cooked and refrigerated before shipping) dog foods have become increasingly common in recent years. All

---

* Artificial sweeteners and especially Xylitol, used in sugar-free candy and gum, are worse than addictive—they're toxic. In general, transparency is as excellent a quality in a dog food manufacturer as it is in a government agency. If you can't get answers to any questions you might have about a product, either via e-mail or phone, it's likely wise not to feed that product to your dog.

claim to provide a healthy and balanced diet in a convenient, nonperishable (or at least long-lasting) form.

Not all are as balanced or as convenient as others—nor as appealing to every dog. I tried one of the dehydrated varieties, only to discover that, after adding water, I had to wait 10 minutes before the food reconstituted itself. Used to more immediate gratification when he spots me puttering around the kitchen, Frankie waited impatiently for dinner. Upon finally being presented with a doggie version of grits, he turned up his nose at the bowl. I'm not sure whether he wanted something to sink his teeth into, or whether it was an olfactory issue; Frankie refused to discuss it.

But that's hardly a statistically significant sample (except to me). I'm told that dog food rolls—which have the consistency of liverwurst—are so tasty that bits are used as training treats, and that they're the only thing some finicky pups will deign to dine on.

All in all, these products run the gamut in taste, texture, and Rex appeal. If you decide to use them in a diet plan, it's always best to check with your vet—and with the *Whole Dog Journal,* which has reviewed many of them. At a minimum, make sure you choose a food that's labeled "complete and balanced."

42. AREN'T BETTER-QUALITY FOODS MUCH MORE EXPENSIVE THAN BIG COMMERCIAL BRANDS?

The difference in price between a high-quality company's food and a major manufacturer's "premium" product isn't all that significant, but with the big companies you're also paying for advertising, whereas the smaller businesses generally spend more on the product and less on pushing it. And for some niche varieties, such as freeze dried and dehydrated, you're eliminating the water weight that bulks up other products—and inflates their prices. To economize on high-class kibble, buy in bulk and store the unused portions in sealed bags in a cool, dark place.

More to the point: pay now or pay later at the vet. Crappy* food is bad for your dog's health. Period.

43. HOW DO I AVOID FOODS THAT MIGHT BE RECALLED?

With difficulty. If possible, restrict yourself to products that list the country of origin of their ingredients and the location of the manufacturing plant.** When I realized that one of my (former) favorite brands of chicken strips, sold by a small company promoting its healthy products, were produced in China, I stopped buying them. The company claims that they spot test each batch and I'm pleased about the disclosure of the factory locale—which is more than many large manufacturers do—but I think I'll wait until they move their production to the United States in case some melamine slips through, thank you.

In September 2007, a few months after the massive pet food recalls, Congress passed the Food and Drug Association's Amendments Act (FDAAA), which mandated new standards and improved labeling within two years. Don't hold your

---

* It also tends to produce more crap, literally. The lower the quality of the food—especially the cheap, corn-based varieties—the less of it is absorbed by the dog and the larger and softer the stools. I admit this isn't terribly well documented in scientific literature, but I suspect that's because of a dearth of poop-size correlation studies. That hasn't deterred me and several alert friends from judging other dog owners' feeding practices by the size of their charge's turds.

** Unfortunately, this remains voluntary rather than mandatory, even when it comes to human food—so fat chance that dog food is going to be better regulated any time soon. In spite of efforts of consumer groups, as well as state agriculture and ranching associations, legislation mandating country of origin labeling has been stalled time and again. Pet Food Politics: The Chihuahua in the Coal Mine, by Marion Nestle, is a fascinating—and frightening—look at this aspect of food safety oversight or, rather, the lack thereof.

breath for anything to happen. In 2008, a year after the FDAAA's passage, instead of starting from scratch and writing new, more effective legislation, committee members dredged up the old laws and added huge loopholes. And, as we went to press in 2009, the early warning and notification systems mandated for pet food recalls were nowhere in evidence. To find out about recalls, your best bet is to check the ASPCA's website, www.aspca.org.

44. GIVEN ALL THE MANUFACTURING PROBLEMS, WHY CAN'T I JUST PREPARE FOOD AT HOME FOR MY DOG?

You can. There's a common misconception that dogs should never eat human food. More accurately, your dog shouldn't subsist on table scraps or eat scraps that are unhealthy for them.*

Which is a comparatively recent development. Dogs did fine on scraps when they lived on farms. The first prepared dog food was a response to city life: In 1860, James Spratt created Patent Meat Fibrine Dog Cakes to provide London's shipyard pups with more nutrition than they could get from scavenging hardtack (biscuits). Many of the mass-prepared dog foods that followed in the United States continued to feature meat, if not prime cuts, until the Depression. With the rise of highly processed dog food after World War II, any real health benefits were sacrificed for convenience and low cost (especially for manufacturers). The fact that so much human food is equally unhealthy explains why table grazing isn't an ideal nutritional plan for your pup.

---

* Tops on most current lists of things to avoid are chocolate, raisins, grapes, avocados, onions and onion powder, garlic and garlic powder. Seeds and stems of most fruit are verboten, too, as are—surprise, surprise—alcoholic beverages and moldy, spoiled, and fatty foods.

I came to home cooking for Frankie reluctantly, because I tend to avoid cooking for myself. When I learned about the problems with many commercial dog foods, I simply switched to better brands. Then Frankie was diagnosed with diabetes and my vet prescribed a kibble in which "chicken meal by-products" was the sole ingredient that seemed to have even a remote connection to the natural universe. And none of the good-quality brands fit the recommended high-fiber/no-grain/low-fat bill.

I won't go through the saga of seeking a home-cooked diet tailored to a small, insulin-dependent dog. Suffice it to say, the two holistic practices I consulted were long on supplements and general advice—and, in one case, on testicle-site massage (see question 27)—and short on actual portion sizes and ingredient proportions. It took lots of independent research and many weight/age/exercise level calculations to come up with the ideal Frankie formula. Diets that need to be adjusted for other health problems, or those geared toward modifying behavior (which I discuss in Chapter 6), pose challenges that may make home cooking extremely difficult if not impracticable.

Even if your dog is healthy, deciding to prepare meals in your kitchen requires more than throwing some good ingredients together. For an adult, you'll want to create a diet that includes, roughly, 25 to 30 percent protein, 30 to 35 percent fat, and 30 to 35 percent carbohydrates (preferably complex);* in the appropriate portion size for her weight and exercise level.

My favorite source for balanced recipes is the amusing and informative *Becoming the Chef Your Dog Thinks You Are* by

* Caveat: This formula is not uniformly accepted. Some studies have shown that dogs have no carbohydrate requirements at all. It's like the debates over Atkins, South Beach, the food pyramid, polyunsaturates ... —ever-shifting and far beyond my level of expertise.

Micki Voisard,* a self-described Master Dog Chef (www.
dogchefs.com). Other recommended books include *Dr. Pit-
cairn's Complete Guide to Natural Health for Dogs and Cats,
Home-Prepared Dog and Cat Diets* by Donald Strombeck, and
Real Food for Dogs by Arden Moore.

Another option, though not an inexpensive one, is a nutritional consultant, who will tailor recipes to your dog. Reputable businesses, including The Possible Canine (www.
thepossiblecanine.com) and Veterinary Nutritional Consulta-
tions Inc. (www.petdiets.com), will not send the diet directly
to you, but will fax it to your vet for approval. Health research
geeks—if you keep the Merck Manual on your nightstand, that
means you—might start with the National Research Council's
Nutrient Requirements of Dogs, available from The National
Academies Press (books.nap.edu), a dense, comprehensive
resource intended for professionals.

45. WHAT ABOUT THE BONES AND RAW FOOD DIET?

The premise of this "evolutionary" regimen—introduced by
Australian veterinarian Ian Billinghurst in *Give Your Dog a
Bone* (1993)—is to put your pup in touch with his inner wolf.
Eschewing grains and focusing on raw meat, vegetables, eggs,
and other foods found in nature (mostly; somehow yogurt
found its way in), the diet seeks to replicate the preprocessed
menu of canids past. And the program deems chomping on
raw bones so atavistically enjoyable as to enhance a dog's
immune system.

Even setting aside the issue of the considerable differences
between today's domestic dogs and their ancestors, I can't
help but be suspicious of an eating plan that has BARF as
its acronym. Why risk being mistaken for a dog bulimia

---

* It was at one of Voisard's cooking classes—sadly, no longer offered—that I first
  learned about the evils of most packaged commercial foods. They're also detailed in
  her book.

manifesto? With a simple word substitution, the diet's advocates could have had the clever, nonpuke referencing—not to
mention vocabulary-enhancing—BARC, for Bones and Raw
Comestibles.* Too late; it's mine now.

Having gotten that out of my system, as it were, BARF has
many appealing aspects, not the least of which is its avoid-
ance of cooking. Many breeders swear by the plan and one
vet I spoke with said many of her patients thrive on it. The
diet has become so popular that it's spurred the creation of
local co-ops that buy meat in bulk from butchers, as well
as of lines of packaged, dehydrated food and supplements
(which would seem to defeat the whole dancing-with-wolves
premise).

Probably the most controversial aspect of the diet in its pur-
est form—aside from the care that needs to be taken to avoid
salmonella**—is the question of whether the benefits of
chewing bones, even raw ones, outweigh the risk of having
them splinter and lodge in the esophagus or digestive tract.

As it happens, Frankie is on a modified BARF diet. He eats
mostly lightly cooked vegetables, meat, fish, and eggs, no
grain. Bones are not an issue. Pre-diabetes, when I used to
give him uncooked marrow bones, he licked out the tasty,
high-fat centers, chewed off the bits of meat left on the
outside, but only nibbled desultorily on the bones themselves before losing interest. I guess he's more evolved in
the bone-gnawing department than he is in the eat-while-
you-can arena (see question 36).

---

* If you think "comestibles" sounds pretentious, consider that on the official BARF
website, www.barfworld.com (barf world? really?), the acronym also stands for
Biologically Appropriate Raw Food. Not very snappy. I haven't yet hammered out the
details of my own oven-free diet but I figure a good name is half the battle.

** As many advocates of the diet reasonably argue, people prepare raw food for their
families in their kitchens all the time and manage to avoid poisoning themselves and
their loved ones. And salmonella is present in lots of processed foods, too, as anyone
who wasn't in a coma during the peanut butter fiasco knows.

46. DOES MY DOG NEED SUPPLEMENTS?

It depends on the diet she's following—and how you feel about supplements. I try to eat enough vegetables, fish, cheese, and chocolate and drink sufficient quantities of red wine to fulfill my daily vitamin and antioxidant requirements without resorting to pills. Because Frankie can't follow the same regimen, I give him calcium and a multivitamin. Those who buy packaged dog food—as opposed to home cooking— shouldn't need to add nutrients; that's what AAFCO approval is meant to ensure. And as with the human varieties, pet supplements aren't regulated. If you're thinking about buying mineral-enhanced designer water for your dog, I have some oceanfront property in Tucson that might interest you, too. But that doesn't mean I necessarily recommend unfiltered tap water. As has been widely reported, the water systems of several cities throughout the United States are laced with pharmaceuticals—the result of people flushing expired drugs down the toilet. You really don't want to dose your dog with even small quantities of antibiotics—or with Viagra.

47. HOW DO I GET MY DOG TO BE LESS PICKY?

I've heard it suggested, including by vets, that if your dog is "gaming" you by not eating his food, stop feeding him for a few days. When he's hungry enough, he'll eat whatever you put in his bowl.

I don't question the effectiveness of that advice. It would doubtless work on a picky child, too. So what if the snubbed food has the potential to make your dog sick—which is why he didn't eat it in the first place? You've proved your domi-nance over a starving pet.

True, dogs can be manipulative. Frankie sometimes barks and rushes to the front door, even if there's no one there, hoping that after I've left my desk, I'll head to the refrigerator for a snack—and give him one, too. (Okay, I admit it worked a few times; I'm on to him now, though!) But doggie deception is generally geared toward getting food, or getting more of it, not acquiring a particular kind. Trust your pup. Dogs have— and develop—food sensitivities and allergies. If yours isn't eating the comestibles you give him, try different comestibles (yes, I'm trying to accustom you to that word, the better to popularize my future raw food diet).

It could also be a question of your dog not liking a food's texture or smell; the latter often occurs as dogs grow older and their sniffers get weaker. Adding a small portion of something more desirable to kibble often does the trick.

Food switching can upset a pup's stomach if you don't do it gradually, and it's essential to check with your vet if your dog has lost his appetite. But dogs are, literally, creatures of habit, and don't mind eating the same thing every day if they like it.* So if your pup balks at his dinner, he's trying to tell you something. Please listen.

---

* The Whole Dog Journal *recommends alternating between three or four high-quality foods, changing them off slowly every few months, to provide your dog with different protein sources and nutrients. They advise against including "novel" proteins such as kangaroo, however, as these should be reserved for food allergy control tests (and, besides, may make your Jack Russell Terrier jump even higher than he already does).*

48. IS IT OKAY TO GIVE MY DOG DIET PILLS IF SHE'S TOO HEAVY?

Sure, if you have money to burn and don't mind turning your dog into a guinea pig. Doggie diet aids are relatively new, but if they follow the path of the human variety, they're likely to prove harmful down the line. My prescription: feed your dog less—or better—and exercise her more. Canned pumpkin, for example, falls into the "better" category. It's a low-calorie—if you don't make the mistake of buying the sugar-filled kind—high-fiber food that makes your dog feel full. By substituting pumpkin for half a portion of kibble, many owners have seen their pups shed unwanted weight. Because it's naturally sweet, most dogs really love it, too.

If your dog knows how to raid the refrigerator, get a good lock for it. If she's able to pick the lock, get her a job as a dog actor (or thief). She'll get plenty of exercise—and you'll have added incentive to keep her trim by avoiding overfeeding.

Of course, if she has an actual glandular problem, then pills are okay.

49. MY DOG HAS HALITOSIS. WILL THE BREATH MINTS I'VE SEEN IN PET STORES HELP?

They'll help for about as long as they help your alcoholic uncle Dave cover his whiskey breath at family gatherings. In dogs, bad breath is generally caused by tooth and gum problems. Forget the faux-candy cover-ups; you need to get to the source of your pooch's halitosis by checking with a vet or veterinary dentist.

50. SO DO I NEED TO BRUSH MY DOG'S TEETH?

I'm afraid so. Some 75 percent of dogs—the number is higher in small dogs—suffer from periodontal disease by the time they're two or three years old. It can be headed off, to a large extent, by beginning to brush in puppyhood. I avoided brushing during my first few years with Frankie because, well, I didn't want to. His teeth are short but sharp, and I suspected he'd be opposed to having me put anything besides food or toys into his mouth. Besides, I never let him chew gum or eat sugary snacks.*

The bottom line: At one point in my quest for a diabetes-friendly diet, three different vets looked into Frankie's mouth, clucked, and recommended a professional cleaning, suggesting that, if unchecked, the bacteria massing in Frankie's gums might course through his immunity-impaired bloodstream and attack his heart, brain, lungs, and liver. Doggie dentistry and muzzles being mutually exclusive, the procedure requires general anesthesia, which makes it very

---

* Tooth-brushing also seemed to go against the dogs-are-evolved-wolves grain. But has anyone done a study on tooth decay in prehistoric wolves? They may have passed a predisposition to periodontal disease down to their canine kin. According to one study, 80 percent of dogs, especially small ones, have some degree of gum disease by age three. We know that working dogs often break their teeth carrying hard objects— and that they can now get metal crowns.

expensive. And by the time I got him to the dentist, he had to have seven teeth removed.

To ensure that Frankie won't end up capable only of gumming his food—or look even more like a little redneck pup than he already does—I became a teeth-cleaning fool.

Note: Don't fall for advertisements for anesthesia-free cleanings outside of a vet's office. For one thing, the dangers of anesthesia have been greatly exaggerated; under proper monitoring, the risk is minimal. More to the point, nonprofessional plaque removal is worse than no cleaning at all. Periodontal disease starts below the gum line—an area that's painful to reach. The purely cosmetic cleaning that a groomer can legally perform may fool you into thinking that your dog's teeth are healthy when they aren't. Moreover, such necessary adjunct procedures as x-rays, polishing, and flouride rinse have to be done under anesthesia in order to be effective and safe. The cost? Again, pay now or pay later. In dogs, as in humans, scientists are increasingly finding links between periodontal disease and heart disease and other life-threatening conditions.

If you're wondering how to convince your own dirty-mouthed dog to submit to this process, here are some tips.

START SLOWLY AND STAY UPBEAT

Getting your dog used to having a foreign object that isn't food or a toy in his mouth is more than half the battle. Dip your finger into low-salt beef or chicken bouillon, let your dog lick it off, and then rub your bouillon-soaked finger gently over a small area of teeth and gums (luckily, you don't have to get inside the teeth; your dog takes care of that with his tongue).

Act excited, like this invasion of dental privacy is a treat, until you've managed to convince your dog to be equally enthusiastic. Expect it to take a few days, minimum.

ADD ABRASIVENESS

In surface, not attitude. Continue to be enthusiastic while, with a finger now swathed in bouillon-soaked gauze, you rub the teeth and gums with small circular motions.

SWITCH FROM BOUILLON TO TOOTHPASTE (OR RINSE OR GEL)

But not to your brand, which can upset your dog's stomach; dogs can't be trained to rinse and spit, so yours is going to swallow whatever you use. Mint isn't a preferred taste, in any case; canine toothpaste flavors range from malt and chicken to wild salmon.

Note: This step can be eliminated and you can continue to use low-sodium bouillon if your dog likes it. It's cheaper and, except for the small amount of salt, doesn't have any potentially unhealthy ingredients.

SWITCH RUBBING INSTRUMENTS

When your dog is used to the toothpaste, get him accustomed to whatever instrument you plan to use. Options include toothbrushes, dental sponges, and dental pads. I like the finger brush, a kind of rubber finger puppet with a rough surface at the tip. It gives you more control, or at least the illusion of it. If you use a brush, work the toothpaste down deep into the bristles; otherwise, your dog will just eat the toothpaste and skip the uninteresting part of the process.

MOVE INTO VIRGIN TOOTH TERRITORY

After you've got your dog used to the toothbrush or tooth-brush surrogate and toothpaste in a small part of her mouth, keep adding teeth to the procedure, until you get them all.

The good news: dogs' teeth are too close together to require flossing.

51. ARE CHLOROPHYLL BONES AND OTHER CHEWS AS EFFECTIVE AS BRUSHING?

No. According to the Veterinary Oral Health Council (VOHC www.vohc.org), brushing is the gold standard. Although the VHOC does approve some products in the following cat-egories as complementary to dental health, the cure may be worse than the disease—especially because, unlike brushing which is interactive by definition, not everyone remembers the importance of supervising a chewing pup.

CHLOROPHYLL BONES

The best known of these, Greenies, were taken off the mar-ket temporarily a few years ago because they caused fatal blockages in several dogs. The chewed pieces reconstituted themselves, gluelike, in their stomachs. Greenies were re-formulated to eliminate that problem, but these and similar products can still cause choking if dogs eat pieces that are too large—this usually occurs when owners ignore the size/weight recommendation—or don't chew them sufficiently. That could be said for any food, of course, but it certainly defeats the teeth-cleaning goal in this case.

RAWHIDE

These addictive leather strips may pose multiple threats to your dog. Toxic chemicals used to cure and strip hair from the animal hides may include arsenic and formaldehyde, and carcinogenic dyes, such as Red 30, are often used to color the hides and give them flavors such as bubble gum and teriyaki. Because dogs spend hours chewing these strips, they get maximum exposure to these toxins.*

Consider, too, that rawhide expands to four times its size when soaked in liquid. This means that if your dog swallows large enough pieces, they can expand and cause intestinal blockages—just as the original Greenies did.

That's not to suggest you should never use rawhides, as they're a good way to keep mouthy pups from chewing even more potentially dangerous—or valuable—stuff. Just choose the type you buy carefully. The Whole Dog Journal emphasizes the importance of sticking to rawhides made in the United States, and especially recommends those made by Wholesome Hide in Chicago.

ASSORTED BODY PARTS

Hooves, tendons, ears, snouts, knuckles, and even penises ... if there's a cow or pig part that can be sold as a dog chew, it's on the market. These anatomical edibles are promoted as all-natural, and many of them are indeed just desiccated versions of the originals. Others, especially those produced in countries outside the United States, contain dangerous preservatives. Conversely, if they're not preserved well enough, they may contain salmonella bacteria. And the good brands are expensive.

Everyone has a gross-out threshold. I reach mine with food items that bear too close a resemblance to their origins. In addition to meeting that criterion, hooves are very hard, which means dogs can crack their teeth on them. I'm told, moreover, that they smell really pungent, as do bull penises,

---

* If your dog's potential health problems don't convince you, you cold-hearted creature, consider the damage to your house: it's impossible to get the dye from a colored rawhide chew off anything it touches.

a.k.a. bullysticks.* Much to my relief, Frankie wasn't interested in the pig's ear I once brought home—being a rescue,
he could be kosher for all I know—and I've avoided similar
items ever since.

---

* *These don't actually resemble penises, but Frankie is a sensitive pup. I'm sure he*
  would intuit their origin and be offended.

CHAPTER 5
GROOMING AND ACCESSORIZING

52. IS GROOMING ONLY FOR POODLES* AND OTHER FROU-FROU DOGS?

Definitely not. These procedures, key to your dog's health and well-being, shouldn't be confused with fancy hairdos. If the word grooming sounds too metrosexual, think of it in automotive terms: body work (maintenance of the overall exterior, or coat) and detailing (focusing on the smaller but essential parts like feet, ears, eyes, and teeth).

53. DO I HAVE TO GO TO A PROFESSIONAL GROOMER OR CAN I GROOM MY DOG MYSELF?

It depends on the type of dog you have, the way you'd like her to look, your income, and the steadiness of your hands with clippers for hair and nails. Most people let a groomer take care of some things and do others themselves.

I have no problem, for example, brushing and bathing Frankie and giving him impromptu haircuts, but he's small—which means resistance is futile—and his fine, wavy hair lends itself to the tousled Benji look. Expressing his anal sacs and trimming his toenails? No, thank you.

At a minimum, though, you should brush your dog regularly, the better to stimulate the skin and allow natural oils to circulate. Brushing or combing sessions are also an opportunity to peer at your dog's pelt and, while you're there, check out her ears, eyes, and teeth. Mats (as matted hair is known) and knots can cause skin irritations and, eventually, infections. If you don't pay attention, fungi and insects—and, in very large

---

* Poodles have gotten a bad rap. Not only were these super-smart dogs once renowned as water-fowl retrievers, but their much maligned coifs were job related. The natural coats of standard "pudels"—German for "splashes in water"—are thick and water absorbent. To help the dogs move more swiftly through water, portions of fur were shaved, with the chest and vital organs left covered to protect them from the cold. The silly looking topknot allowed the owner to tie a strip of colored cloth to the head, the better to spot the speedy retriever from a distance.

dogs, squirrels and small children—may take up residence in tangled hair. So keep up with regular body-monitoring and hair care before problems become severe, painful, and costly to resolve.

The best time to get your dog accustomed to brushing and clipping is during puppyhood, but if you adopt an adult dog who isn't used to being groomed, go slowly, introducing different procedures one at a time and associating each with treats and praise. Many dogs have sensitive areas, especially their paws—what's with that, anyway?—so tread particularly carefully in those places.

If you're trying to decide just how hands-on you want to get, pick up a comprehensive guide like the *Everything Dog Grooming Book* by Sandy Blackburn or a demonstration video.

54. DO I NEED SPECIAL EQUIPMENT TO TAKE CARE OF MY DOG'S COAT?

To a certain degree, yes. But it doesn't have to be expensive. Most of the required hair rakes, combs, and brushes cost less than $10. Even with clippers, which are pricier, there's a point of diminishing returns. If you don't invest about $250 or $300 for a sharp, smooth-cutting version, you're likely to give your dog a hairdo that borders on animal abuse (or at least fashion victimhood). But high-status, high-tech clippers that run as high as $650 won't produce better results; in less-than-skilled hands, their cuts can still be unkind. The good news for anyone put off by the term grooming: some of the equipment is very macho sounding—for example, the FURminator, which many vets recommend.

Each type of coat requires a different set of tools—and a different frequency of use. And mixed breeds may have hair* that doesn't follow any strict rules for care. The following is just a rough guide of what to expect, going from highest to lowest maintenance.

LONG-COATED

These breeds, which include Afghans, Maltese, and Yorkies—essentially, all the ones that look like trotting mops at dog shows—and several types of spaniels, require constant attention because their fine, cottony hair gets matted and tangled easily. Ideally, you should run a fine-tooth metal comb through your dog's hair every day, even if it's just a quick sweep. Using a wire slicker brush on the hair a few times a week is also recommended, as is seeing a groomer every other month.

DOUBLE-COATED

These furry and hairy pups, which include Pomeranians, Shelties, Huskies, Collies, and Akitas, may fool you: their coats can look fluffy and neat but hide a matted mess underneath. That's why you have to go below the surface to the undercoat, using tools like a grooming rake or the aforementioned FURminator, a blade tool. You should brush weekly, at least, and visit a groomer every three months. Not only is this a good plan for your dog, but it'll help with the housekeeping (see the following question regarding shedding).

Note: One of the reasons that both long-haired and double-coated dogs need to be brushed, combed, and/or raked

---

* The debate about whether there's a difference between dog hair and fur rages on. It's usually agreed that hair grows constantly and doesn't have a seasonal shed, while fur is thick and has an undercoat. However, there are so many exceptions as to render these distinctions meaningless. Rather than get into follicular nit-picking, as it were, I'm stipulating that if it's short and thick, it's fur, if it's long and silky, it's hair. Think of the popular (at least with women) categories for human males: if it's on the head, it's hair; if it's on the back, it's fur.

regularly is that you don't want their coats to get to the point where they need to be shaved off entirely. Coats don't always grow back properly, so your dog may end up with endless bad hair days. Worse, while waiting for her body-cover to reappear, your pup may suffer from sunburn, windburn, and insect bites—not to mention the itchiness and irritation of prickly hairs. Short haircuts are fine for warm weather but don't overdo the clip-jobs.

CURLY/WAVY

Caring for this type of coat can range from the simple brush-and-trims I give Frankie, whose hair is not only wispy but naturally short (it stops growing beyond an inch or so), to the constant vigilance required for poodles and other water dogs with thick, curly mops that grow long and wild if not kept in check. On the plus side, these dogs have only one coat, so what you see is what you get. Brushing with a pin or slicker brush, raking, and then combing carefully usually takes care of the preliminaries, to be followed by clipping as straightforward or fancy as you like.

SHORT-COATED

These trim-haired pups, among them, Boxers, Pugs, Pit Bulls, and dogs with giveaway names like German Short-Haired Pointers, require only a rubber mitt or coarse washcloth for coat care, which is more like a rubdown—more good news for the macho—than a hairdressing session.

55. WILL TAKING REGULAR CARE OF MY DOG'S HAIR PREVENT SHEDDING?

No. Shedding is a natural, ongoing process for dogs, just as it is for humans. As anyone who's ever worn a black sweater or jacket can attest, regular brushing and combing won't prevent a bit of hair divestment. But some dogs, like some people (say, males of a certain age), shed more than others. The double-coated breeds are the worst offenders; many send forth so much hair that they practically create an alternative dog,* giving rise to the expression "blowing coat."

The only consolation is that this mass exodus of hair is seasonal, and therefore predictable. Increases in daylight and warmth in spring signal certain canine brains to release hormones that spur the dogs' undercoat to grow and push off their topcoats. A similar, though somewhat less dramatic, version of this process occurs in fall, when the pups know they need to grow a new winter coat (unlike kids who always require back-to-school wear, at least dogs do it themselves and never demand designer labels).

A few things can interfere with regular shedding. If you keep a dog who's genetically programmed to shed seasonally indoors most of the time, he may not register natural changes

---

*   Some people spin dog hair and weave or knit it into clothing, which I find intensely creepy—not the least because, should I be complimented on them, I wouldn't want to admit that I was wearing a scarf or sweater made from my dog. If you disagree, Kendall Crolius's Knitting with Dog Hair: Better a Sweater From a Dog You Know and Love Than From a Sheep You'll Never Meet, might be for you.

in temperature and light and therefore shed year-round. Copiously. Which proves it's a bad idea to mess with Mother Nature. Using human shampoo on your dog can dry her skin, and even dog shampoos with perfumes that are not from natural sources may result in hypersensitivity—additional causes of shedding. Excitement and stress can trigger hair-loss hormones, too (if you can't get your dog to meditate, consider Doga). In rare cases, excessive shedding may be a symptom of a health problem, from a food allergy to a thyroid imbalance. If your dog isn't the shedding sort or if the off-season hair loss seems excessive, check with your vet.

Still, if shedding can't be prevented through grooming, it can be managed by it. It's far better to have hairs concentrated on a brush or on a newspaper than randomly faux-carpeting your floor or creating furry throws for your couch. You can entrap large swathes of your dog's coat with a rake or deshedding tool, even—or especially—during her molting season.

There's always the vacuuming fallback. See Chapter 9 for details.

56. WHAT DO I NEED TO KNOW ABOUT WASHING MY DOG?

First, I'd like to address the question of who benefits from a dog washing. I've read that dogs love being clean. Ha. If they're so keen on personal hygiene, why do dogs persist in rolling around on bird carcasses? Why do they resist our efforts to wash them, and show no interest in washing themselves (licking their privates doesn't count)?

If they really wanted to be clean, they would be cats.

Brushing and other types of waterless—aside from a little spritzing with conditioner—grooming generally suffice to distribute oils, prevent skin irritations, and remove bugs. In short: the prime reason to subject your pup to full body immersion with a soap product is that you don't want her to stink.

Which is understandable. Dogs tend to invade your personal space, and even the most malodorous don't take hints or even direct instruction about bathing. But not all dogs smell bad. Short-haired dogs and lap dogs, for example, need fewer baths than long-haired breeds who enjoy romping outside in disgusting debris, or than retrievers and other pups with oily, water-repelling coats that get, well, rancid.

So bathe your dog regularly if you like—with a few caveats, noted later. Just don't delude yourself that you're doing it to make her happy.

LOCATION

Bathing is, at best, a messy process. The larger the dog and the more unwilling she is to get wet, the messier it will be. To avoid shampoo residue from remaining in your dog's fur and drying her skin, you need sufficient space and water pressure for a proper rinsing. A small indoor plastic tub won't cut it.

Some people have enough room and enough disposable income to build separate washing and rinsing bays for their dogs. Others manage to lure their pups into a shower, fit them into a sink with a showerhead attachment, or hose them down in a backyard. A lot of pet stores now have self-service bathing stations, and many cities even have dedicated dog washes (the one in my neighborhood is called Dirty Dawgs).

Wherever you decide to shampoo your dog, remember the rinse cycle is key. Be aware, too, that your dog will shake herself vigorously after these ablutions. No matter how well you've toweled her, flying water will be involved.

PREPARATION

Assuming you're doing this at home, lay out the shampoo—don't forget that the human variety can cause doggie dandruff and other skin irritations—and old towels in advance.

Have two or three towels available, lest you end up even wetter than you're likely to be anyway. Here's a key to the proper size for your needs:

- Hand or bar towels—teacup breeds only

- Standard size—fewer than 25 pounds

- Bath size—25 to 75 pounds

- Bath sheet—75 to 100 pounds

- Family size beach towel or Army surplus blanket—more than 100 pounds

PROCEDURES

Brush the tangles and small creatures out of your dog's coat first, clipping out intractable mats and sticky stuff such as tar or bubble gum.

Wet your dog thoroughly before applying shampoo. Work in small circles near the skin so as to avoid hair tangling. Then rinse, rinse, rinse, making sure all the soap residue comes out. Try not to get any water in the ears.

Pat your pup down well with towels, then let her air dry (but not in the yard or anywhere near dirt; it's a well-known fact that there's a magnetic attraction between just-washed dogs and soil). You can use a doggie dryer or a human one that doesn't employ heat—never, ever use one that does—but unless your dog is very small you'll be exhausted by now. Your job is done. Let nature take its course.

FREQUENCY

As needed—let your nose guide you. Monthly is fairly standard. Washing more than once a week is unhealthy—though not necessarily for your dog, if you do it correctly. Rather, too-frequent canine bathing suggests you've got a cleanliness fetish. Find a hobby or take your germ-phobia out on your house.

57. WHAT OTHER PARTS OF MY DOG DO I NEED TO WORRY ABOUT?

I've already discussed the need for dental care in Chapter 4 (see question 50). Paws and ears are also prime grooming targets.

PAWS

Not all dogs need their nails trimmed. Some file their own nails by walking or running on hard surfaces. Pups that don't pound the pavement, however, and small breeds that don't weigh enough to successfully self-file need pedicures. Over-long nails can get caught in carpets or clothing, or become ingrown and infected. They can also throw off a dog's gait—which, for older pooches, can exacerbate arthritis pain.

A dog's nails should be trimmed about once a month to just short of reaching the floor.* It's not a bad idea—theoretically, anyway—to combine trimming with bathing because nails are softer after being submerged in water. Of course, your dog might not want to put up with two annoying procedures on a single day.

---

* Except for the nails on the dewclaws—the vestigial digits that sit farther up on the leg and thus don't reach the floor. These should nevertheless be trimmed because they have a tendency to get caught on things. In fact, such an accidental snagging may be the first time you become aware that dewclaws even exist. It took several friends to talk me down from my conviction that Frankie was a mutant when I discovered he had these stunted appendages—and on every paw, yet.

Nail trimming is neither easy nor risk-free, especially for dogs that have black, nontransparent nails. Clip off too much and you'll literally cut your dog to the quick—the pink, tissue part of the nail that contains nerve endings and blood vessels galore.

Clippers, which come in scissors- and guillotine-style varieties, were the most common way to trim nails until recently, when electric files came on the market. These strike me as less potentially dangerous—especially than the Marie Antoinette-model clippers—because you have to proceed slowly. On the other hand, your dog may not take kindly to being approached by a mini buzz saw.

I'm not going to go into detail about trimming your dog's nails because I don't want you try this on your own the first time; ask your vet or someone experienced to show you. That said, if you're going to ignore my advice, have a styptic pencil or a Kwik-Stop powder on hand to staunch the blood flow in case you hit a vein.

But nails aren't the only paw parts to require your attention. Don't forget to check your pup's footpads. Dogs often get burrs, stones, or other foreign objects caught between their toes. Carefully remove everything that doesn't belong. Dry, cracked pads, which may be caused by walking on hot concrete, should be treated with a moisturizer (or prevented with shoes; see question 60) but not yours, because your dog will try to lick it off. Ask your vet or a pet supply store to recommend a safe one.

EARS

Floppy eared dogs and dogs that don't shed are particularly prone to ear infections, the former because germs like to breed in the dark, moist areas created by those big flaps; the latter because hair growing in the ear canals often mixes with wax and forms unwanted earplugs. Constant pawing at the ears* may be a sign that your dog has a health problem (or that he wants you to turn down the stereo). By the time your dog's ears smell bad and ooze, they're already infected and require professional care.

No matter what type of dog you have, peer into his ears at least once a week. Many preventative powders and cleaning solutions are available for breeds that are predisposed to ear problems; ask your vet for recommendations. Do not, I repeat *not*, stick Q-tips in your dog's ears. Think of the damage that people manage to inflict on themselves with these swabs, and then consider that your dog won't be able to tell you if you've reached down too far—or that he might suddenly turn his head, which could have the same effect. A punctured eardrum is far worse than an ear infection.

Removing hair from a dog's ears is not dissimilar to removing it from a human's ears;** plucking and trimming implements are required. As with nail-trimming, this is a procedure best left to a groomer or attempted only after you have been instructed by a professional.

ASSORTED CRUD-COLLECTING AREAS

Most dogs get a little crust in the corner of their eyes, just like we do when we get up in the morning. They can't remove it with their paws like we can, however. I—and, if we're being honest, many of my dog-owning friends—just pick the stuff off with our (clean) fingers, but it would be wrong for me to suggest something less than hygienic, so use a moist cotton ball. This is also the treatment for the tearstains to which

---

* If you've walked your dog in a dry, grassy area, this and headshaking might indicate that a foxtail has entered his ear or nose. These seed heads, particularly common in California, can be very dangerous because they have tiny, sharp barbs and can migrate into the brain. See your vet right away if you think your dog might have picked one up.

** This is an excellent reason for people who need to trim their ear or nose hair to get a dog. As with other body-function embarrassments like farting, you can blame the dog for the presence of these instruments in your house.

many small, light-colored dogs are prone. Reddened, swollen, or itchy eyes, on the other hand, might be caused by allergies, conjunctivitis, or parasites; if the whites of your dog's eyes aren't, be sure to get them checked.

And—sorry, but yuck—jowly, wrinkly pooches such as Chow Chows, Bulldogs, Basset Hounds, and Shar-Peis need to have their skin folds wiped out regularly to prevent dermatitis or fungal infections. Use baby wipes or cotton swabs with hydrogen peroxide, then dust with unscented talcum powder.

58. WHAT SHOULD I LOOK FOR—AND LOOK OUT FOR—IN A GROOMER?

Anyone with a water source and a pair of clippers can put out a dog-grooming shingle in many states, no license required. But these seemingly benign professionals—after all, groomers aren't practicing medicine, right?—can pose grave dangers to your dog.

Among the things that you should look out for:

CAGE DRYING

Similar to clothes dryers without the rotation, cage dryers are glass-fronted boxes into which your dog is enclosed and blasted with air; some units offer separate cages for more than one dog. They're good for groomers, who can increase the volume of their business by working on other dogs while yours is drying, but not so good for the dogs, who can't escape (and who can't sweat; they can only pant to try to cool themselves off). If the temperature is turned up too high and your dog is left in too long, she can dehydrate and die.

As a result of several canine fatalities, a few states are trying to outlaw cage dryers.

Some reputable groomers contend that they use only the un-heated fan option, even going so far as to remove the heat coil. Others say they never set the temperature above 80 de-grees and never leave the room. Maybe so, but why tempt fate? At the least, these enclosures are likely to frighten the bejeezus out of your dog.

UNAUTHORIZED TRANQUILIZING

If a groomer is sufficiently gentle—and doesn't use scary equipment—your dog shouldn't need to be tranquilized. Some clients allow their dogs to be sedated, which is their preroga-tive (see later discussion), albeit one that should be used very sparingly. Some groomers, however, don't ask—and don't tell. That constitutes practicing medicine without a license and without permission from the patient's guardian. If your dog is allergic to them, tranquilizers can be as dangerous as cage dryers.

OVERLONG STAYS

Imagine waiting in a doctor's office all day with other equally stressed out patients, many of whom are yelling at each other and at the receptionist. Loud, frightening noises are coming from places that you can't see. And oh, yes, you can't stretch your legs or get up to go to the bathroom. Why would you want to subject your dog to that? A good groomer should stagger appointments so that your dog is worked on and available to be picked up as quickly as possible. Two hours, total, is ideal; up to half a day is reasonable. A full day—fuggedaboudit. Taking your dog to a groomer isn't, as some owners seem to regard it, a way to get free dog sitting.

If you're just getting your dog's nails clipped and/or anal glands expressed, it's reasonable to ask if you can wait; it shouldn't take more than 10 minutes, total. I never leave

Frankie at a groomer; he's a shy little guy and it would make us both unhappy.

So how do you find a good groomer, then?

GET A REFERENCE

Ask your vet, neighbors, friends, and family members for recommendations.

TOUR THE FACILITIES

Drop in unannounced and say you're looking for a new groomer and want to look around. If you're not allowed into the area where the grooming is done, leave.

Things to look for while you're checking the place out include:

- Cleanliness. Not only of the cages but also of the entire room. You don't want your dog rolling in other dogs' dirty, discarded hair.

- Spaciousness. Your dog should have plenty of room to move around in a cage, maybe read a few magazines, while waiting his turn to be groomed.

- Kindness. It seems like a no-brainer, but the staff should act as though they actually like dogs (yours in particular).

- Up-to-date equipment. Aside, of course, from cage dryers. Check also to see that the hand dryers don't use heat. The latest models, geared specifically toward pet grooming, work with cool air alone.

TALK TO THE STAFF

Don't only chat with the owner, but also with the groomer who's likely to be working on your dog. Because a license may not be required, you can't ask a staff member to produce one, but you can ask her about the type and length of her experience and what inspired her to choose the profession ("I just got out of the slammer and this was the only job I could get without references" is not among the correct answers). You can also ask about her grooming philosophy; she doesn't have to quote Emmanuel Kant, only tell you how she feels about what works best for her canine charges.

In the end, trust your gut—and your dog. If you're feeling uneasy and your usually calm, outgoing pup starts shaking and whimpering, try somewhere else.

You, in turn, have a responsibility to be honest about your dog—both with a potential groomer and with yourself. Of course you have the best dog in the world, but face it, others might (irrationally, naturally) find him intimidating. When a groomer discusses possible scenarios with you—how your dog responds to his feet being touched, for example—tell the truth. Some dogs are generally polite but go ballistic when confronted by strangers with shiny instruments. A good groomer will tell you whether or not she is equipped to handle the type of behavior you describe—or ask you if it's okay to use tranquilizers. These should be a last recourse, and you should only use a type to which you know your pup is not sensitive. Still, if your dog is in danger of being condemned as a public health hazard, sedation might be in everyone's best interest.

Alternatively, and even if you have a perfectly well-behaved pup, you may want to have a groomer come to you; this is an especially good option for fearful and elderly dogs (and owners). Among other benefits, it eliminates waiting, cage drying, and unobserved meanness. Mobile grooming vans are common in many cities, but they generally require a water hookup, which means they can't service urban high-rises or even many suburban apartment complexes. If you don't mind a temporary mess, most groomers who are willing to make house calls would also be willing to use your bathroom as a workspace, and even to clean up afterward.

59. SO SUE ME, I LIKE A FROU-FROU DOG. WILL NAIL POLISH AND THE OCCASIONAL COLOR RINSE HURT HIM?

I don't think they'll inflict psychological damage, if that's what you're asking. Many dogs love the attention they get when they're well turned out. And they really can't tell whether you're laughing at them or laughing with them.

I wish I could be as certain about the health issues involved. According to some vets, fast-drying nail polish brands especially formulated for dogs are safe. Although dogs don't bite their nails, I would definitely avoid using human varnish, which contains (even more?) toxins.*

I haven't found any permanent hair dyes that are recommended for canine use. Plant dyes such as henna that wash out should be safe, though reddish-brown is not an especially sought-after hue. Food coloring is fine for special occasions, too. If at all practicable, however, I would suggest a hairpiece instead. Some especially designed for pups—see wigglesdogwigs.com, for example—not only come in bold colors, but allow your dog to change her hairdo with her mood.

60. WILL MY DOG HATE ME IF I DRESS HIM?

Dogs aren't shy about letting you know if they hate you; they tend to let their teeth do the talking when they're really upset. Dogs who are less categorically opposed but still

---

* *Browsing Internet forums on the topic, I came across posts that read, in effect, "I've used human polish on my dog for years and it hasn't killed her." "Not dead yet" is hardly my idea of a ringing endorsement.*

unwilling to be clothed might squirm vigorously or run away. So if your dog allowed you to dress him in the first place, expressing only mild irritation or even approbation, you can assume you're in the clear. Dogs don't hold grudges in any case.

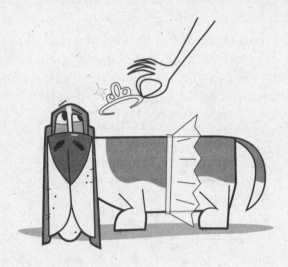

Some purists think dogs should never be dressed, including humorist Fran Lebowitz. "If you are a dog and your owner suggests that you wear a sweater ... suggest that he wear a tail," she wrote.

I think that's a bit harsh. Few dogs earn their keep these days. A little harmless couture modeling in exchange for room and board seems reasonable. Of course, it would also depend on the outfit and the occasion. If you're dressing him for Santa Barbara's annual Big Dog parade, say, your dog would be in good company, and probably enjoy the interaction with other natty canines. But itchy attire like frilly tou-tous wouldn't be appreciated under any circumstances, a fact to which your pooch will doubtless alert you.

Functional clothing is another matter entirely.

If you have a dog, such as a Chihuahua, who's bred in a warm climate, a light wrap for a night chill is always appropriate. And in parts of the Southwest where asphalt temperatures can rise higher than 110°F during the day, booties aren't a fashion statement, but essential protection for sensitive footpads. Cold climate dogs also benefit from being shod. Not only do shoes keep pups from slipping on ice and from getting snow between their toes, but they serve as a buffer against the caustic products used to melt the white stuff. And sometimes clothing is dictated by work conditions. Police dogs in Dusseldorf, Germany, wear blue plastic shoes to protect their feet from the broken glass created by revelers in the city's many pubs and caught between beer-soaked cobblestones. Why blue? To color-coordinate with the police uniforms, of course.

CHAPTER 6
BEHAVING AND BONDING

61. I'M OKAY WITH MY DOG'S BEHAVIOR. WHY BOTHER WITH ANYTHING BEYOND HOUSETRAINING?

Let's see ...

TO KEEP YOUR DOG ALIVE

You may think your dog would never run out into traffic—until she does, at which point it's too late to wish you'd trained her to respond immediately to a recall. And if your dog bites a stranger or two, no matter what the provocation, there's a strong possibility she'll have to be euthanized. Training may not reverse your dog's impulse to chomp down when frightened, but it can help you read the warning signs and to keep her out of potentially dangerous situations.

TO KEEP THE LINES OF COMMUNICATION OPEN

Good training has nothing to do with blind obedience or turning your pooch into an automaton. Rather, its goal is to let your dog know what you expect from her so she can behave accordingly and vice versa. The better you understand each others' signals, the less frustrated with each other you'll be, and the deeper, and the more deeply rewarding, your relationship will be.

TO KEEP YOUR FRIENDS

Just because your dog's eating habits don't disturb you, others won't necessarily appreciate your pup jumping up on the table and grazing from their plates at dinner parties. (Of course, depending on your cooking skills, she may be appreciated *under* the table, performing the classic function of dispatching unsuccessful culinary efforts.)

TO KEEP YOURSELF AND YOUR DOG ON YOUR TOES

I'll talk more about the importance of mental exercise in Chapter 7, but ongoing training is a great way for both you and your dog to stay alert and connected, and for the two of you to spend quality time together.

TO KEEP OTHERS IN AWE

Most people, even those who like dogs, don't realize the reach of canine capabilities, so it's easy to impress them with pretty much anything beyond the basics of "sit" and "stay" and "down." Don't think of skill demonstrations as parlor tricks but, rather, as payback for the endless displays of toddler abilities you've had to endure. If your dog turns out to be more impressive than your friends' toddlers,* all the better (as long as you refrain from gloating).

62. DO I HAVE TO SEND MY DOG TO A FARM OR MONASTERY TO GET HIM TO DO MY BIDDING?

There was a time when trundling your dog off to a countryside kennel for a month or so to get him trained—a practice inspired, in part, by the Monks of New Skete and their tough love *How to Be Your Dog's Best Friend* (1978)—was very popular. Although no longer as trendy, entrusting your pup to a professional who returns him to you with better manners hasn't been eliminated from today's bag of training tricks.

If you're feeling overwhelmed by the rowdy canine stranger who's come to live with you, or your family is hopelessly confusing your dog by giving him mixed signals, remote training may be tempting. In theory, it's supposed to work like rehab, to get your dog to establish better habits away from bad influences and under professional guidance. But even aside from

---

* *Teach your dog to go to the bathroom on command—no, it's not an urban legend; I've seen it done—and you'll earn the undying envy of new parents.*

the considerable expense of most of these boarding programs, they have several limitations.

THEY MAY CREATE UNREALISTIC EXPECTATIONS

You might imagine your dog will come back from the country a changed canine, a perfect pup who will intuit your every wish. So what if your noisy Manhattan apartment doesn't resemble the verdant fields where your dog learned to hustle when summoned? She'll figure it out. As with all overblown expectations, a failure to meet them can lead to disappointment and frustration, perhaps even greater than what you experienced before your dog was trained. Poor you, poorer pup.

THEY'RE USELESS WITHOUT FOLLOW-THROUGH

Unless you and your family are trained to replicate the signals used to convey information to your dog, including the cues and body language you need to avoid, any benefits of the program will erode over time. If the regimen doesn't include extensive home follow up, it's not worth the investment.

THEY'RE WORSE THAN USELESS IF BADLY HANDLED DURING PRIME TRAINING TIME

If you send a puppy away during the optimal window for socialization and training (between 8 and 12 weeks) and the process is bungled, you've blown a key education opportunity. Yes, your dog can learn—and unlearn later, but not as thoroughly or effectively as when he's at the most impressionable age. It's akin to the difference between absorbing a foreign language as a kid immersed in the culture and learning it from classes and tapes as an adult.*

---

* *That's not to suggest you should give up on older rescues. Frankie, who was five when I got him, is far from uneducable. (Of course, it helps that he's exceptionally bright).*

YOU HAVE LESS CONTROL THAN YOU DO WITH OTHER TRAINING PROGRAMS

Because your dog is at a remote—if not undisclosed—location and you will likely be discouraged from visiting during the first week, minimum, you won't have a clue about what's going on. For all you know, your dog could be crated most of the day or forced to dance the tango in a traveling circus (and you won't get any of the proceeds). It's essential, even more so than with other programs, to check the credentials of the school and trainers and to scope out the premises, even if all come highly recommended.

THEY OFTEN RELY ON HARSH—AND DISCREDITED—TECHNIQUES

Even the Monks of New Skete, who resurfaced on Animal Planet's *Divine Dog* show, no longer emphasize physical correction in their training methods.

63. BUT DON'T I HAVE TO DOMINATE MY DOG TO MAKE HIM BEHAVE?

Ah, yes. If you don't discipline your dog harshly as soon as he does something you disapprove of—say, attempting to jump on your bed—he will eventually take over. Everything. Before you know it, he'll be turning your Barcalounger into a Barker-lounger, commandeering (or eating) the remote control, and forcing you to watch *Meercat Manor, Mr. Ed,* and other nonspeciesist shows.*

There's truth to the popular notion that you have to establish yourself as the "alpha" to earn canine respect; as with kids, dogs need structure. But being a leader doesn't require domination through physical force. Nor does positive training, the alternative route to being recognized as the household CEO, mean coddling.

---

* But not Lassie, *because of the bad example it sets of unquestioning canine obedience.*

Advocated by most mainstream dog trainers these days, guiding behavior through reward rather than punishment first came into the public eye in the 1950s, when it began being practiced on large marine animals. Unable to use bodily coercion to make whales and dolphins do their bidding, trainers employed food and the sounds associated with providing it (whistles, and in some cases, clickers) instead. This system proved—and remains—consistently effective. Anheuser-Busch doesn't have to worry about irate crowds at SeaWorld demanding their money back because Shamu and pals refuse to perform.

Why the delay in applying these methods to dog training, then? To distill a somewhat murky history, studies of captive wolf packs were interpreted to suggest that these positive techniques wouldn't carry over to hierarchical canids. The degree to which dogs and wolves have parted ways is still a hot topic, but most ethologists (animal behaviorists) now agree that our domesticated pups don't exhibit the behaviors on which harsh training methods were based.*

Theories aside, the more that professional dog trainers used the reward system, the more they discovered that it worked, that it worked long-term, and that it didn't pose dangers to owners—as punishment-based training often does. Performing the much-publicized alpha role, for example, is a good way to provoke a dog into biting your face off.

Positive training is not a simple, one-size-fits-all approach. Its specifics vary, depending on the individual practitioner—and on the individual dog. Frankie, for example, won't eat when he's in an unfamiliar situation such as a training class—a

---

* If you're still wed to the whole "we're living with wolves in dogs clothing" notion, consistency demands you follow it through to its logical conclusion: human pack leaders need to hunt prey or scavenge road kill, eat it raw, and regurgitate it into their dogs' mouths. Come to think of it, that could be the premise for a great cross-promoted reality show—Survivor: Animal Planet. I'm going to see if I can get Frankie to set up some pitch meetings for me.

reaction to stress he certainly didn't get from emulating me—but responds enthusiastically to praise and chest scratches. So rewards for good behavior don't have to involve food and/or an accompanying clicker sound.

Methods of discouraging undesired behaviors vary, too. They range from the redundant sounding "negative punishment"—which simply means withholding positive cues—to distracting your dog with a command when he's doing something off-topic. The bottom line: although it's based on sound scientific principles, effective positive training is also an art honed through a knowledge of dogs in general and yours in particular.

64. CAN TRAINING BE LEARNED ENTIRELY THROUGH BOOKS AND DVDS?

Only if you plan never to take your dog out of the house and introduce her to new people and situations. If you've got a puppy, it's especially crucial that she work with a professional who can quickly assess her temperament—strengths as well as weaknesses—to help her get the most out of a training class.

Your temperament needs to be assessed by a professional, too. Even the most ambitious autodidact* won't succeed with books and tapes without getting somebody knowledgeable—and neutral—to evaluate the follow-through. You may think you're being consistent, but while your mouth is praising "Good dog," your body language may be bellowing "That's the last liver treat you'll see unless you shape up, bud."

That said, getting a background in reward-based training techniques and watching them performed effectively will positively reinforce your decision to give your dog confidence and make him revel in your presence rather than playing on his insecurities and making him fear you. A prime place to get

---

* *Someone who, unlike me, doesn't buy instructional DVDs only to end up using them to prop up an uneven leg on the dining room table.*

started is www.dogstardaily.com, which posts an array of excellent free demonstrations and downloads, including books and videos by the always entertaining Ian Dunbar, veterinarian, certified dog trainer, and site cocreator. The site's blogs, written by such top behavioral experts as Nicolas Dodman and Patricia McConnell, are very informative, and the recommended products section can lead you to other star talent in the field (including Suzanne Clothier, Jean Donaldson, and Karen Pryor, among my favorites).

65. HOW CAN I FIND A GOOD TRAINER?

Dog trainers can hang out a shingle without any qualifications— and a lot of them do. Some ways to separate the mystery meat from the filet mignon include:

SEE IF THEY'RE JOINERS

Membership in the Association of Pet Dog Trainers (APDT; www.apdt.com), devoted to continuing education and "dog friendly" techniques, is a good sign. A search by zip code will lead you to APDT members in your area who have been accredited by the Certification Council for Professional Dog Trainers (CCPDT; www.ccpdt.org)—which means they've performed at least 300 hours of training within the last five years and have undergone a lengthy standardized exam in everything from equipment to ethology.

Listed next, uncertified members of APDT who have established themselves as dog trainers may or may not be highly qualified—you just have to pay an entry fee to join the organization—but, at minimum, membership indicates an awareness that training is a profession, not a hobby, and suggests at least a cursory interest in networking and knowing the state of the training art.

CHECK WEBSITES

The fact that a trainer has bothered to create one is a good start. Other things to look for include the following.

Currency

I know, not everyone updates their websites regularly (guilty!) but if you're referred to an address that says "We're looking forward to getting this site up in early 2007" you've got to worry about the trainer's seriousness and organizational skills.

Attitude

One website of an APDT member I came across disses everything from "university veterinary behavioral programs" to "food-bribery trainers" and group classes. I wouldn't want to put my dog in the hands of someone so insecure that he needs to disparage the methods of others instead of just explaining the virtues of his own approach. In my experience, such humans often exhibit fear-based aggression.

Unwarranted claims

Be wary of anyone who guarantees results within a certain period of time—or guarantees results, full stop. All you can expect is that a trainer do her best, using tried and true methods, for your dog. These methods may not succeed as a result of factors completely unrelated to a trainer's skill— breed temperament or illness, to name just a couple.

CHECK OUT A CLASS (WITHOUT YOUR DOG)

If you ask to observe a class and the trainer refuses to let you, that's a red flag right away. But even when you're allowed to sit in, you might not have a context for what you're seeing. Laughter, excited squirming (on the part of the dogs), and tail wagging (ditto) are all good signs; raised tones, sharp commands, and long silences are not. Whatever your impressions, be sure to follow up at the end by asking class members what they think. Few will be shy about sharing.

BE CLEAR ABOUT YOUR GOALS

Unless you know what you want, it's impossible to determine whether a particular trainer can give it to you. For puppies, it's pretty much everything—i.e., life preparation—but for older dogs you need to be a lot more specific than "I want her to behave." A good trainer should be able to help you focus if you don't have a sense of your options, and let you know if you're being unrealistic about an objective—say, getting your dog to put a roller in his mouth and paint your house.

TRUST YOUR GUT

Assuming your gut is connected to your heart rather than to your machismo or machisma lobe. When I first got Frankie, I took him to S., a trainer highly recommended by two dog-loving friends. She was nice, smart, and clearly fond of dogs, but the first purchase S. required in preparation for the small dog class was a choke chain. The Frankie-size version was teeny, a wisp of a metal string, but it made me queasy.* I ventured a few questions about the more positive techniques I'd heard about, but S. pooh-poohed them. And, after all, I was paying—and paying well—for her expertise. I figured I should defer to it.

In the end, waste of money notwithstanding, I was lucky. Frankie was too stressed out by the presence of the other small dogs—a snooty clique of Yorkies and Dachshunds—to learn much of anything, but neither did he learn to fear me.

---

* *As it turns out, with good reason. See question 70.*

And although I failed Chain Jerking 101,* I discovered that my instincts about how to treat my new friend were sound.

66. WHAT ARE THE BENEFITS OF GROUP VERSUS INDIVIDUAL LESSONS—AND WHAT CAN I EXPECT TO PAY FOR EACH?

For puppies, group classes are the key to learning how to play well with others and how to inhibit biting instincts. It's more complicated for older dogs, some of whom will benefit from peer pressure more than others (as my experience with Frankie can attest). Only dogs without major aggression or fear issues are good candidates for the group experience—at least if they haven't had some advance individual training.

As with every service, rates vary depending on where you live, but $150 to $300 for a series of six group classes is a good ballpark figure. Individual sessions can range from $50 to $150 for an hour but you can expect progress fairly quickly (although completion may take longer). If you don't see the slightest difference in your dog's behavior after two or three sessions, look for someone else.

67. CAN I LEARN TO SPEAK "DOG" AS WELL AS A DOG TRAINER?

Sure—and you'll doubtless be better at the local dialect spoken in your house. All you have to do is keep your eyes and ears open and avoid shutting down the lines of communication. A dog that growls, for example, is trying to tell you something, whether it's a fear-based, "Leave me alone," or a possessive, "Hey, that's mine." It's in your best interest to investigate what's behind the growl rather than attempt to suppress it. If

---

* *At least as applied to Frankie; I suspect some of my exes might disagree about my chain-jerking skills.*

you discourage self-expression, next time your dog might go straight to bite, do not pass snarl.

But it's a two-way street. You not only need to decode your dog's signals, but to be aware of what you're telling him, whether deliberately or inadvertently.

The good news is that dogs can learn hundreds of words in our language, including ones we don't intend to teach them— thus the common phenomenon of people in doggy households spelling to each other, "I'm just going out to the c-a-r." They can even get past our ineptitude. We tend to treat our canine charges as we do foreign exchange students, repeating words, adding more of them, and speaking louder when we're not immediately understood. But if we take the time to understand what our dogs are saying and to transmit our wishes more effectively, a surprising amount of information can be exchanged.

Books such as Patricia McConnell's *For the Love of a Dog* and *The Other End of the Leash,* and Stanley Coren's *How to Speak Dog* go into the topic in great and fascinating detail, and Sarah Kalnajs's DVD *The Language of Dogs* adds visuals. The following is just a quick sketch of some of the basics.

WHAT YOUR DOG IS TELLING YOU

When you spend time with a dog, his barks are pretty easy to read, whether low and mean, high-pitched and excited, or persistent, almost rhythmic, demands for attention. Frankie recognizes my ability to tune out this last kind, so he occasionally fakes the more urgent variety.

Body language, on the other hand, may be more difficult to decode. Some moods and their indicators include the following.

I'm stressed and afraid

Some signs of high anxiety will be obvious even to dognoramuses: a tail between the legs, ears pinned back, cringing, shaking, and pacing. Others may be less familiar, such as the out-of-the-corner gaze that leaves the whites of the eyes showing, known as whale eye. And some cues are ambiguous. Yawning might mean sleepiness, for example, lip licking and drooling could be food-related, and lying on the back could indicate a desire for a belly rub. Put a few of these mixed signals together, however, and add a bit of submissive peeing to the back flip, and you can bet your dog is scared and/or upset.

I'm ready to rumble

Along with the obvious snarling, teeth baring, and growling, a dog that's on edge is likely to give a hard, cold stare (not dissimilar to the one you might get if you're caught checking out someone other than the person you're with); stand stiffly; raise her ears (if you have a breed that can do that); and hold her tail rigid (ditto). She might also raise herself up on her toes to look bigger and tougher, unless she's Great Dane-size, in which case, why bother?

Play with me, please!

Anyone who's ever taken yoga will recognize the play bow as the downward-facing dog position (far easier for Frankie to assume and maintain than it is for me). Dogs who feel frisky and eager to engage will look relaxed, tail wagging lazily, maybe even a full body wiggle. If you think your dog is smiling, you're probably not imagining it; loose lips and an open mouth are part of the picture. Finally, gentle nose nudging and pawing—or dropping a favorite toy at your feet—are clear signs of playfulness.

WHAT YOU'RE TELLING YOUR DOG

Dogs are far better at reading our body language than we are at reading theirs—thus their successful adaptation to our world over the millennia and our (not unwarranted) belief that they can intuit our moods—but the gap between canid and primate is often difficult for them to bridge nevertheless. And because we primates don't often bother to learn canid, the results include the following.

Unintended rudeness

Approaching a dog directly and staring straight at him, for example, is considered an act of aggression; so is leaning down and patting him on the head. Hugging? Sudden movements? Sticking your hands in his face? All are intrusions into canine personal space, and they may cross over from annoying to downright scary. That's why kids, with their sudden, impulsive movements, so often frighten dogs—and why dogs bite them.

Confusion

Sometimes dogs believe they're speaking the same language as we are and don't understand why they're not getting their point across. Say your dog is barking and you yell at her to shut up. She's thinking, "Oh, you're making a loud noise, too. Good—let's keep it going," but is puzzled by your rigid posture and the tension around your mouth.

This is where Dogspeak 101 comes in handy. You'd be amazed at how quickly even simple attempts to communicate—ignoring the barking and rewarding a brief bout of silence, for example, or blinking and yawning to calm a stressed dog—can yield results.

68. I'VE HEARD TRAINERS CAN HELP WITH SOCIALIZING AND DESENSITIZING. WHAT'S THE DIFFERENCE?

Socializing is the process of introducing dogs to the scary, complex world they're going to be sharing with us, and showing them how they're expected to behave in it. Ideally, puppies should be exposed to lots of different people, dogs, noises, and sights in their first 12 weeks so that nothing will faze them later on. One way to accomplish this—in addition to taking them to training classes—is to arrange for small groups of friends to come over and handle your pup* while watching loud action movies and/or listening to heavy metal. If you can get your pals to put on hats and carry umbrellas, you get bonus points. It's fun, plus any outlay for beer and pizza (or whatever inspires your particular group) will be more than compensated for by having a friendly, well-balanced dog.

Desensitizing performs mop-up duty for dogs who have not been properly socialized, helping to ease their fears. (These fears can also be breed-based or spurred by a single frightening episode.) Methods vary, depending on the source of the fear and its intensity,** but they don't include "flooding," or full-on immersion—the canine equivalent of shoving an arachnophobe into a room full of spiders. Nor do they include babying. If you try to soothe a fearful dog, it only confirms her view that there's actually something to be afraid of.

---

* It's best, however, if your friends avoid dropping her too often. Dogs, especially young ones, are resilient but not indestructible.

** Some cases require medication, at least initially. See the following question.

Typically, the dog's desensitizer remains calm and confident while carefully exposing the pup to the source of her anxiety—whether it is shiny shoes, pugs, or men in black—and creating new, positive associations with it. Here again, professional guidance and the help of a few friends are essential. It shouldn't be hard to find people willing to role-play—wearing shiny shoes, say, or dressing in black—and toss treats around. Who doesn't love a chance to be silly for a good cause? Borrowing a pug might be more difficult but by no means impossible, and most pugs are happy to cooperate; they're a helpful, fun-loving lot.

69. ARE THERE DOG SHRINKS—AND, IF SO, HOW DO I KNOW IF MY DOG NEEDS ONE?

Specialists who treat dogs for mental health issues—as opposed to dogs who earn advanced degrees in psychology*—are called behaviorists. This is a vague, blanket term; it would be like teachers, social workers, psychologists, and psychiatrists all going by the same title. One way to distinguish between the different people who call themselves behaviorists is by fee structure: the highest rates go to those who have the credentials to wield a prescription pad.

But that's relative. Dog trainers may give themselves the behaviorist label so they can charge more than instructors who don't know enough to claim it. Consultants with an M.S. or Ph.D. in a field of animal behavior have a far more legitimate claim to the behaviorist name, especially Certified Applied Animal Behaviorists (CAABs; www.certifiedanimalbehaviorist. com); in addition to an advanced degree, CAABs are required to have five years of field experience. These experts don't all do training—they haven't necessarily majored in dog—but can usually provide knowledgeable referrals.

---

* *Or dogs who are experts in manipulating human behavior.*

The top dogs in the canine mental health hierarchy are veterinarians who are board certified in the specialty of behavior. This is a relatively new discipline; in 2008, there were fewer than 50 members of this elite group in the United States. Check the website of the American College of Veterinary Behaviorists (www.dacvb.org) to see if there's one near you. Renowned among their ranks is Dr. Nicholas Dodman, a best-selling author who founded the Tufts University Animal Behavior Clinic and pioneered the field of animal behavioral pharmacology.

Reading Dodman's *The Dog Who Loved Too Much* is one way to tell if your dog needs a shrink. Documenting case studies of canine patients who *really* have problems, from obsessive tail chasing to severe separation anxiety, this book will give you perspective on your dog's mild shyness or occasional temper tantrum.

Most of the time, you'll know if your dog is in imminent danger of harming herself or others and thus in need of expert help. But there are gray areas, including behavioral changes that seem to come on suddenly, that may leave you wondering whom to consult.

If you suspect your dog may have a problem that's beyond the scope of a regular trainer, start by checking with your vet. Some obsessions are breed-related, for example, and sudden aggression could be caused by pain from an undiagnosed illness. And any veterinary generalist—or layperson who watches Animal Planet—will tell you that exercise is the key to canine mental health. Diet may make a difference, too. It's worth asking your vet if feeding your dog less protein might lessen her aggression, for example.

A behavior modification program, such as desensitization for fear, guided by a trainer with good credentials, might be the logical next step.

Finally, there are drugs. If you're hesitant to go there, consider that ...

- A variety of antidepressants and antianxiety drugs were tested on animals before they arrived on the human market. It's only fair that animals get to benefit from them, too.

- If a beloved relative or friend had a mental illness, you wouldn't question the use of medication, would you? (If you would, you're incorrigible.) Why deprive your dog of something that might improve her life—and your lives together?

- Your dog doesn't have to become drug-dependent. Some antianxiety drugs, for example, might break a cycle of obsession, allowing behavioral therapy to kick in.

- The new class of "smart" drugs in the Prozac family won't deprive your dog of his personality as sedating Valium-type drugs commonly did in the past.

🦴 We often drive our dogs insane by depriving them of their natural environments and making them do odd things to please us. If you've tried other routes, why begrudge them a bit of chemical relief?

That doesn't mean we should start drugging our dogs for acting doggy—as we dose our kids with unneeded Ritalin, say. As with everything in life, it's a question of balance.

70. WHAT TYPE OF GEAR DO I NEED TO KEEP MY DOG UNDER CONTROL?

In the best of all possible worlds, your impeccably trained dog would walk calmly by your side without a leash and never jump on—or hump—your visitors. And we would have lasting peace in the Middle East. In our actual universe, we need restraint equipment to help keep our inquisitive pals from endangering themselves, from driving us nuts, and from falling into the clutches of animal control. Call it the hardware to the software of training.

Naturally, there's no consensus on which restraints are the most humane and the most effective. On one end of the spectrum are people who believe that dogs shouldn't wear neck collars of any kind because they're ineffective and/or harmful; on the other are those who regard shock collars as the only way to get dogs to toe the line. Similarly, opinions on crates range from considering them safe havens to condemning them as doggie lockups.

Any restraint is only as benevolent as the dictator who administers it, and even cruel tools can be used responsibly by skilled practitioners. Still, the following assessments take into account the ease with which well-intended but inexpert handlers can screw up and harm their pups. In theory, most of these should be used for training only; in practice, many of them end up as permanent accessories—which is another reason to avoid some of them in the first place.

NECK COLLARS

Time was when few questioned the neck collar as the anchor for a leash and ID tags. In recent years, however, the efficacy of trying to guide dogs by the neck—with or without pain—has come under dispute. The base of the neck doesn't have many nerve endings, the argument goes, which is why bridles are used to get horses moving and nose rings rule in camel caravans.

The neck collar's effect on canine health has been examined, too—especially for small dogs. The neck may not have nerve endings, but it can be damaged by constant pressure.

Nevertheless, the following items still dominate the racks at pet supply emporia.

Buckle or snap-on (a.k.a. flat) collars

The standard default collars, these don't do anything but hang around the neck. They're fine for dogs who don't tend to yank or pull vigorously.

You'll be spoiled for choice in this category. To start with, get something adjustable, especially if you have a rapidly growing puppy. A collar should be loose enough for you to slip two fingers* into, tight enough so your dog can't escape; three fingers usually leaves too much room. (Wait until your dog relaxes a bit to perform any digital measurements.) The smaller the dog, the wider the collar should be in proportion to her neck; otherwise a swift tug can turn it into a garrote.

After that, anything goes. People who wouldn't dream of dressing their dogs get their sartorial kicks with

---

* One finger is advised in the case of toy breeds—and measurers who have huge, sausage-fingered hands.

collars—metro-bling, natty nautical, Guatemalan-weave, ethno-chic ... you name it and it's available in a real or virtual pet boutique. Most collars simply make a fashion statement, but others are also utilitarian. If you walk your dog at night, for example, consider neckwear that glows in the dark or pulses flashing lights.

Choke or slip collar

As the less frightening of its aliases suggests, rather than buckling or snapping together, this collar slips around a dog's head. Whether consisting of chain link or nylon, it bears a metal ring at each end. One is inserted through the other and attached to a leash. When the dog tugs, so does the collar. If put on or used improperly, the slip collar may choke your dog ceaselessly (and, if it accidentally catches on something, fatally). If put on and used properly, it chokes your dog selectively by applying a quick, snapping pressure that serves as a correction.

If you don't have a problem with booby-trapping your dog's exercise, perhaps you'll be dissuaded away from this collar by the fact that even correct use may be harmful to his health. According to one post-mortem study, some 92 percent of dogs on whom choke chains were used showed damage to the soft or hard tissue of their necks. In particular, the trachea and esophagus of small dogs were vulnerable. Additionally, choke chains can put pressure on the ocular nerve, bringing on glaucoma in breeds that are susceptible to it. They may also create pulmonary edemas in brachycephalic dogs—the ones with pushed-in faces.

Partial slip or Martingale collar

Originally designed for dogs with heads narrower than their necks, such as Greyhounds, these collars combine the flat collar and the choke chain—only without the choking part.

That is, they only tighten slightly when a dog pulls on them, which keeps the collar from slipping off. Usually. That's one of the disadvantages of this type of restraint: if the flat part that goes around the dog's neck isn't adjusted to exactly the right length, leaving a gap between the rings to which the leash is attached, or if the dog backs up suddenly, he can slip out of the collar (and not just partially).

Prong or pinch collar

Ouch! This collar consists of a series of wide chain links, each with metal prongs that turn inward toward a dog's neck. More similar to a Martingale than to a full slip collar in that it limits the extent to which it can constrict the throat, this device compensates for its inability to throttle by its potential to inflict sharper and more constant pain. It looks meaner than a choke chain, too—the better to advertise your sadistic tendencies.

Remote collars

The most infamous of the distant-control restraint devices, the shock collar does exactly what its name states. Not only is the idea of wanting to apply even a slight jolt of electricity to your best friend unfathomable to me, but these collars are far from reliable as training tools. For example, you can accidentally set off the current with your TV remote, thus causing your dog to cower every time he hears the opening notes of *Law and Order*.

Less obnoxious, the citronella collar is designed to distract a dog from any unwanted behavior. The most commonly used variety is voice activated, spritzing the pup with an annoying burst of lemon whenever she barks. These collars are not cheap, and finding the cause of the barking would be far preferable, but they're not dangerous, either.* And who doesn't like a quiet, mosquito-free pup?

HEAD HALTER OR HEAD COLLAR

I was taken aback when I first began noticing dogs along the trail wearing these restraints, which wrap, muzzlelike, around the mouth. What could have made all those benign-looking Golden Retrievers turn evil, I wondered—and could Frankie defend himself if one of them escaped? I have since discovered that these so-called head collars, which fasten around the back of the neck and drape over the top of the snout—similar to halters used on horses—aren't designed to keep dogs from biting. Rather, they're intended to keep them from tugging on a leash by replicating the action of mother dogs who lift puppies by the scruff of their necks and/or put their snouts in her mouth. Far from being violent offenders, haltered dogs are simply pups taking direction from a mommy surrogate (you). They can open their mouths, drink, eat, carry toys ... all the things that good dogs are allowed to do.**

Many dog owners swear by these items, sold under such names as Gentle Leader, Halti, and Snoot Loops. They're thrilled by their ability to get their charges to do their bidding without painful coercion. Dogs are not as uniformly enthusiastic; judging by their often-fervent attempts to remove them, halters are probably as uncomfortable as they look. In all likelihood, you'll need to introduce your pup to this headgear slowly, with lots and lots of food bribes.

Two caveats: Although halters are usually safe, if you jerk your dog's head suddenly, you can cause a neck or spine injury. And for obvious reasons, they're not an option for

---

* *Physically, at least. If the barking is caused by anxiety, getting a sudden faceful of spray will only further traumatize your dog.*

** *Head collars are common in Europe, so if you take your haltered dog abroad, you won't be looked at askance. In turn, you needn't worry that vast numbers of Continental dogs have criminal tendencies.*

dogs without snouts—Boxers, Pugs, Brussels Griffons, and so on.

HARNESSES

Dashing through the snow ... Okay, harnesses are not only for sled-bearing Huskies (or reindeer). In fact, small breeds with sensitive tracheas are the most likely to get strapped into these chest cradlers, although most other dogs, and especially escape artists with skinny heads, can benefit from wearing them, too.

In general, because the pressure from a harness is equally distributed, you can't harm any part of your dog's body with them. Even the potential discomfort from chafing straps can be mitigated by felt- or velvet-lined versions, as well as those made from soft nylon webbing.

It's the fact that they're cushy that makes most harnesses unsuited to large dogs who like to go their own way; if you don't let go of the leash, your big lug may have the leverage to pull you down the street, which is embarrassing. The so-called "no-pull" harnesses, however, discourage such behavior by tightening under the front legs and shoulders when your pup tries to haul you away. And those designed so that the leash attaches to the front have the added advantage of getting your dog to move toward you, rather than away from you, to relieve the pressure.

The down side of harnesses? They must be carefully fitted; they have to be used in conjunction with a collar bearing your dog's ID tag; and they can be a huge pain to get on. I bought one for Frankie that has a strap intended to go between his front paws and hug his chest. He prefers to insert both feet on one side while trying to chew on the seatbelt-style plastic buckle that goes around his middle. To be honest, I only use the harness to be PC.* Frankie likes to walk behind

---

* *It's essential for trips to California, where the self-appointed dog police are ubiquitous.*

me, with the rare collar tug therefore catching him on the scruff and not the throat, but I don't want anyone to think that I'm injuring him. If I need to leave the house in fewer than 20 minutes, however, public opinion be damned.

LEASHES*

There are two general types of leashes: the sensible kind and the retractable variety that holds 15 to 30 feet of nylon line in a plastic handle. Too many things can go wrong with retractables to enumerate, but they include: uselessness in case of an emergency (they lock up when they're stretched taut); the ease of getting them tangled in another dog's leash or of having another dog owner trip over them, because they're so thin they're practically invisible;** and frequency of breakage of both the handle and the nylon line. Use the wrong strength, and you can accidentally jerk your small dog off her feet. All in all, if you feel the need to reel something in, go fishing.

Assuming, then, that you're opting for the sensible variety, the main things to consider are length and material.

Length

Four to six feet is a good standard size for both training and general strolling, the shorter length being preferable for urban walking, and especially if street-crossing is involved. For hikes and other outdoor adventures, the so-called long line, a clothesline-type rope that can extend as long as

---

* *You may wonder, as I did, what the difference is between a leash and a lead. I'm sorry to report that I still haven't got a clue. I read somewhere that leash was slang for lead, but I prefer to think that lead is the pretentious Anglophile term, used to summon a dog to go "walkies." Because I've never heard of "lead laws" or "off-lead beaches"—at least in the United States—I've stuck with leash here.*

** *Some retractable "ribbon" leashes are the same width as regular leashes, so the invisibility complaint doesn't apply to them. They have a greater tendency to get tangled than the skinnier kind, however.*

50 feet lets your dog pretend she's off leash. You can step on the leash whenever you want to stop her from forging through the forest, thus crushing her illusion of freedom.

The indecisive and those who enjoy lots of different activities with their dogs should consider adjustable leashes, which have clasps at both ends and several rings that allow you to shorten and lengthen the tether at will or whim.

Material

Leather is the classiest and probably the most user-friendly for the holder, but it's also the most expensive, most liable to be subject to sun and water damage, and most likely to be chewed by your dog.

Chain leashes are sturdy and definitely discourage chewing, but they're uncomfortable to hold unless they have a leather or nylon handle. And if your dog accidentally slaps himself with the leash—ow! (And talk about not PC.)

Nylon and cotton are probably your best bets. They're cheap, durable, washable, and come in lots of colors. You can get one for every outfit—yours and your dog's.

CRATES

I've seen the word "crate" used to refer to everything from snug, hard-sided travel carriers to capacious playpens that afford pups pacing space. It's the in-between size, large enough for a dog to stand up and turn around in but too small for him to transform a separate area into a bathroom, which I'm talking about here.

Properly used, crates are intended to fill in for wolf dens or caves. A dog won't soil the place where he sleeps, the theory goes, which makes these cozy enclosures ideal for maintaining (although not initiating) housetraining. And because canines often need a retreat from irritating *Homo sapiens,* a crate also doubles as a sanctuary.

Nor is there anything wrong with occasionally sending your pal off to chill in a crate during the visit of a dog-averse friend.*

All too often, however, crates are turned into lockups** for dogs who destroy stuff out of loneliness and boredom while their owners are away from home for extended periods. I've said it before, but it bears repeating here: "Bad human, bad human!"

No matter what your intent, you can't stick a dog into a crate cold turkey and expect her not to regard it as punishment. Crate training takes time and effort; the extent of both will depend on your dog's age and her history with confinement. Dogs who come from puppy mills may be used to being caged and find it comfortingly familiar, while those who land at a shelter after living in a home for many years may resist anything that reminds them of the pound.

The Humane Society's website, www.hsus.org, offers a detailed program (click on "pets" and then "pet care") for crate training. Some quick tips for acclimating your dog to her faux den include ...

Associating the crate with good things such as food and toys.

Feed your dog in a crate and keep her toys in it when it's unlocked and she'll begin thinking there might be benefits to entering.

---

* *The longer you have your dog, the fewer you'll have of these, I've discovered. Which is fine. Your new friends will be nicer, smarter, and better looking than the grouches who don't love dogs.*

** *The secured exit, as well as the style or lack thereof, distinguishes crates from doghouses. See Chapter 9 for details on the latter.*

Introducing the crate in a room that your dog likes and that you spend time in.

You don't want your dog to think of the crate as a canine Elba. Put it in a family room, kitchen, or other place where you hang out, so your dog doesn't think he's being exiled or isolated.

Pacing the length of confinement.

Leave your dog in the crate for progressively longer periods of time. Initially, stay in your home while your dog is in his.

Rewarding quiet behavior.

Yes, your dog may initially bark or whine when you lock her in a crate. Resist the guilt that these sounds will inspire, and give your pup a treat as soon as she calms down. If you simply release her, she'll think that complaining is the route to getting sprung.

Limiting the crate's use as a dogsitter substitute.

No matter how used to the crate your dog is, it's no substitute for exercise and company. If your dog is sufficiently tired, she won't need to be confined.

Crates are available in a range of materials, from plastic and wood to wicker, but the most practical are the collapsible wire variety. Not only are these portable, but they can be gussied up to your heart's desire. Dogs like to have a bit of privacy, so you can drape anything over the enclosures, from old towels or sheets to designer covers with acoustic muting properties— and even get coordinating mats to line the bottom of the doggie den. The only problem with some wire crates is the gap between the bottom and the bars, where a dog could catch his paw. A well-fitted blanket or other lining—which you'll likely put in anyway, for warmth and comfort—should take care of that.

And before leaving your dog unattended, always remove any collar with tags that could get tangled on the bars. If your dog survives this traumatic experience—she might, in a panic, try to back up and thus cut off her airwaves—she'll never again consider the crate a refuge.

CHAPTER 7
FUN AND GAMES AT HOME

71. AM I BORING MY DOG?

If you're talking about having caught your dog yawning, the answer is "I couldn't say." As I mentioned in Chapter 6, yawning is often a sign of stress, so your dog might be trying to hint that he needs some space.

Or not. My friend Clare's dog, Archie, is a master of the fake yawn. Archie knows that barking is frowned upon as an attention-getter, but opening his mouth wide and making noises while pretend-yawning always makes Clare laugh and then do his bidding.

And it's possible your dog is sleepy.

But just because his yawns don't reflect on your conversational skills, that doesn't mean you're not boring your dog. Most dogs, and especially purebreds, are hard-wired to perform jobs like guarding, herding, and retrieving.* It was their "will work for food" ethic that got us to share our dinners—and our shelters—with them in the first place. If they're not

---

* *Mixed breeds are excellent multitaskers, the short-order cooks of the dog world.*

allowed to do the work they're suited for, they get antsy. Which is true of humans, too.

Luckily for them, however, dogs don't have to worry about taking dead-end jobs to pay the bills. Give them enough—and suitable—exercise,* and they'll embrace the freeloading lifestyle.

But meaningful work or a facsimile thereof isn't the only thing dogs need to stave off boredom. If anything, dogs are more social than we are, and hate being left alone for long periods of time. It doesn't help that they're barred from getting library cards and accessing the Internet. See questions 75 and 76 for some absentee entertainment suggestions.

72. HOW MUCH EXERCISE IS ENOUGH FOR MY DOG?

It depends. The goal is to tire your dog out or at least take the edge off her restlessness, as well as keep her trim and fit. Some breeds have far more energy than others—you checked before you got your dog, right?**—and all have different exercise needs at different life stages. Ask your vet about the best fitness regimen for your dog.

Your pooch will also let you know, one way or the other, if she's getting enough exercise—perhaps by acting out, or by putting on so much weight that you'll have to keep loosening the straps on her waist-hugging halter.

---

* Many games that are organized for dogs (see question 77) simulate job skills, such as sheep herding and sled-carting. In contrast, few of the real and virtual games humans play bear any resemblance to their jobs, except for professional athlete and mercenary.

** That said, don't stereotype. Dogs are individuals and may not conform to breed profiles precisely, for better or worse. Size and face shape are often good energy-level predictors for mixed breeds, but be prepared for surprises.

She'll also let you know if she's getting too much of a work-out. Panting excessively is one sign (be sure to bring along enough water on your outings). Civil disobedience is another. Having decided that a brisk walk we were taking with my friend Kate and her dog, Kukula, was going on a bit too long, Frankie parked his little butt down in a stolid "I prefer not" pose in the middle of the path. Much to my relief—carrying even 11 pounds can be hard after a couple of miles, especially when they're squirming—Frankie was perfectly fine to walk back on his own four legs. He just wanted to let us know that if we were to proceed any farther, he couldn't guarantee his continuing participation. I wish I were as good at enforcing my limits.

73. WHAT IF I'M NOT FIT ENOUGH TO EXERCISE MY DOG SUFFICIENTLY?

Few humans are capable of keeping up with large, high-energy dogs. This is where props—everything from Frisbees and treadmills to tennis-ball pitching machines—come in. Again, every dog has different interests and capabilities; some like to fetch, others to swim, still others to run with a dog park pack. You just need to figure out what works with your dog's drives, social skills—and size. For example, some large dogs may swallow, rather than retrieve, tennis balls.*

Let physics be your friend, too. If you stand or sit at the top of an incline and toss a stick down it, your dog will burn more calories than if you perform the same ritual on a flat surface.

---

* A prerequisite for many exercise-providing games is your dog's proven compliance with the "drop it" command. You don't want your pup getting too riled up or becoming overly possessive of whatever item is being tossed around or pulled on—or eating it. You may not be able to refine the drop site, however, so dress for the possibility of getting drooly items plopped into your lap or onto your shoes.

And don't forget that, in an off-leash area (or with a very long leash), dog hikes and walks are far longer than human walks. A key theorem of dog math is that for every mile you walk, your dog will cover three or four. This includes the constant returns to show you something disgusting she's picked up or to check that you're still around and on the move before ambling off again to continue her investigations.

Mental exercise is also essential for most breeds—and you don't have to be in shape to provide it. All you need is patience, a sense of fun, and intelligence equal to or above that of your dog.* There are training sessions, for one thing; you might try to teach your dog a new word or trick every day in two or three five-minute sessions. And there are simple games. My friend Jennifer plays hide and seek with her Pit Bull, Beau, and other people I know make their dogs search for treats strategically placed around the house.

And, naturally, you can buy educational toys. In addition to the playthings mentioned in the "Toys" section of question 75, which can safely occupy your dogs while you're away, toys that challenge your dog's mind but require supervision include the soft Puzzle Plush playthings made by Kyjen (www.kyjen.com) and the (mostly) wooden toys in the Zoo Active line by Nina Ottosson (www.nina-ottosson.com).

74. SHOULD I GET A SECOND DOG TO KEEP MY DOG COMPANY IF I WORK LONG HOURS?

Only if you want a second dog. Another dog math theorem is that taking care of two dogs requires more than twice the effort of taking care of one, not half. After that, the amount of labor involved increases exponentially, requiring advanced canine algebra to calculate.

---

* Those who've been outsmarted by their dogs, as I've often been by Frankie, should not be offended by this statement.

And there's no guarantee that the two dogs will get along, your matchmaking efforts notwithstanding. Even if they seem well suited initially, things change. My friend Barbara's two dogs were great friends until Lucy got sick and couldn't play with her pal Halo for a while. After Lucy recovered, Halo declined to resume their relationship, perhaps on the once-snubbed principle. And two dogs in my neighborhood that are left out in their yard all day bark in a cacophony of distress, their misery unmitigated by company.

If you crave canine diversity or want to rescue another dog, more power to you. And your first dog may well be grateful. But if you're primarily motivated by guilt (always tops on my motivation list), divert the extra money you'd spend on food, vet care, and training to some of the pet entertainment possibilities described in the next two questions.

75. HOW CAN I KEEP MY DOG FROM GETTING BORED AT HOME WHILE I'M AT WORK?

Avoiding boredom is crucial for both your dog's well-being and yours. Ennui—not to mention existential angst—might make a dog run around the house chewing stuff up, or it might inspire him to try to escape, convinced you're out there somewhere, ready to entertain him, if only he could find you.

Alternatively, boredom could cause your dog to sleep excessively and mope. Although depression doesn't cost nearly as much as destruction, it is more heart-wrenching. When you're not angry at your pup for wrecking the house, you're open to feeling really, really bad that he's unhappy.

Give your pooch as much exercise as possible before you leave for the day, and avoid making a big exit scene. If you act as though going to work is no big deal, your dog will often respond in kind.

Some possibilities for keeping your dog happy include the following.

AUDIOVISUALS

Leaving the radio, TV, DVD, or CD player on all day may not be energy efficient but if it cheers up your destructive pup, it will definitely be cost effective.

TV/DVD

Dogs are never asked to take part in Nielson media surveys and, as far as I know, no studies have been conducted to determine canine TV preferences. Nor has cable or network programming been geared toward dogs. Animal Planet would seem an obvious channel choice but many dogs, including Frankie, are simply not interested in the shows.* Others try to attack the TV to get at the creatures inside. And still others take a moral stand, preferring only commercial-free broadcasting.

No worries. Several DVDs have been geared toward your pup's viewing pleasure. They include *While You Are Gone,* compiled by Bradley Joseph,** featuring deer, ducks, geese, and wolves. It's well reviewed on its distributor's site, Amazon.com. *Doggy Daycare DVD,* put out by Off the Wall Entertainment (O.T.W.E.; www.otwe.biz), highlights the Puppy Cup, a soccer match between two teams of Golden Retrievers. Go Dog's *Dog Sitter II*—the sequel, of course, to the ever-popular *Dog Sitter*—includes some obedience training clips and sequences of dogs doing incredible tricks to inspire (or shame) your pup.

---

* *In fact, no one really knows how well dogs can see in two dimensions. But you can bet they would probably prefer Smell-O-Vision to even 3-D TV (assuming you could get them to put on the special glasses).*

** *According to Wikipedia, performing with Yanni is one of Bradley Joseph's claims to fame. If you and/or your dog are allergic to New Age music, this may be relevant.*

CDs

Based on observations at many animal shelters and clinics, music does indeed soothe the savage breast. What kind? According to Susan Wagner, a veterinary neurologist, dogs like slow tempos and not a lot of complexity in their compositions. Because they hear at such high frequencies, they also prefer quiet sounds, so *Through a Dog's Ear* (www.throughadogsear.com), the CD that Wagner produced and sells in conjunction with her book on the topic, should be played at a low volume. Of course, no one would blast *Canine Lullabies* (www.caninelullabies.com), created by former songwriter and record producer Terry Woodford, who discovered that what was effective for calming human babies also worked on the furry variety. The reverse holds true, too, according to assertions on Amazon that *Dog Gone Classical Music: Mozart* makes babies mellow out. Also favorably reviewed are the *Music Dogs Love: While You Are Gone* CD, a companion to the DVD (see the previous section); and *Music My Pet,* a classical mix created by Tom Nazziola, the principal performer on Baby Einstein CDs and DVDs.

Radio

I'm not sure that DogCat Radio (www.dogcatradio.com),* a Los Angeles-based Internet streaming station for pets and their owners, can be considered soothing. The play list ranges from disco to Top 40 and Spanish pop, and there's a lot of pet-oriented chat that's useful to owners but not aimed at calming their four-legged charges. That said, if your pup likes an upbeat sound, leave your computer tuned in to the station.

When in doubt, leave your dog tuned in to your local long-hair music station. And lay off the heavy metal. In studies of

---

* *Caveat listener: Although he also has dogs, DogCat Radio founder Adrian Martinez, a former record label president, said he created the station in 2005 because his cat asked him to.*

audio preferences, many hounds howled in protest when they were subjected to it.

TOYS

Not all toys that can keep dogs occupied for long periods* are suited to serve as distractions while you're away. Especially dangerous are those with parts that can be swallowed, from rawhides to toys with squeakers, and anything that can shred or splinter.

The safest picks as doggie distractions (all available in virtual and real pet emporia) include the following toys.

Nonedible chew toys

These toys should be made from material durable enough to stand up to long periods of your dog's attempts to ingest them and be large enough that your dog can't swallow them whole. Popular brands include Dogzilla, Nylabone, Hurley, and Huck. Some have nontoxic flavorings and smells that make them appealing. Be sure to supervise your dog with these products before leaving her alone with them. Some dogs are super-chewers, capable of decimating most products placed in front of them, and you need to know that in advance.

Interactive treat toys

These take the will-work-for-food drive down to its most basic level. The best known—and still tops in its category—are those made by Kong, hard rubber cones that can be stuffed with anything from peanut butter to soaked kibble; many people put half of their dog's morning meal in them. Geared toward dog size, age, and chewing strength, Kongs and Kong-style toys require some coordination—your dog has to hold on

---

* *That's a relative term. Dogs are usually the most upset for the first half hour or so after you leave, so a toy doesn't have to be engaging for more than an hour.*

to them to get at the food—and lots of tongue agility, but not Einsteinian intellect.

More challenging are toys like the Buster Cube and other "busy-boxes," designed so that the treats inside come out of the openings when your dog pokes, paws, and noses them at the right angle. You can adjust their difficulty level when your dog progresses (or regresses). That's true, too, of the Busy Buddy line made by Premier,* which includes the Twist 'n' Treat, a spaceship-style toy that Frankie likes (and has offered to endorse, if the price is right).

76. AUDIOVISUALS AND TOYS DON'T KEEP MY DOG HAPPY. WHAT ELSE CAN I DO FOR HIM WHILE I'M AWAY?

When in-home entertainment isn't entertaining enough for your restless pup, it's time to consider outsourcing his diversion. Dog walkers and doggie daycare are the top options, but play dates and other informal exchanges through networks of local dog owners are getting increasingly popular, too.

Keep in mind that you need to screen potential candidates for dog care as thoroughly as you would candidates for child or elder care—perhaps more thoroughly, because licenses aren't required for canine caregivers in most states and there's little official oversight. Any professional you're thinking of leaving your pup with must love dogs, yes, but they must also know how to handle them—and how to conduct a business. Among other things, that means being bonded and insured and providing you with a service contract.

---

* On one website, Premier's Tug-a-Jug is touted as being made of bulletproof material. I don't find that very heartening. Yes, these toys help hone intelligence, but not even Frankie would be sharp enough to grab the Tug-a-Jug and use it as a shield if he were under fire.

Nor is every dog a good candidate for dog walking or daycare—and I'm not just talking about bullies who don't play well with others. Frankie, for example, refuses to walk anywhere with strangers (a better attribute in a child than it is in a dog). Hanging out with unknown dogs away from home? Not my shy guy.

If you think your dog could benefit, start your search by asking people you regularly see with well-behaved charges at the dog park, dog path, or around the neighborhood. Check with your vet, groomer, pet supply stores, and local shelters. Websites such as Pet Sitters International (www.petsit.com) are good resources, too. And then do your own screening, based on the criteria outlined in the following sections.

DOG WALKER

Dog walkers—who will often have an associated pet sitting business—typically come to your house once a day and take your dog out for 15 minutes to an hour. Usually it's for a group stroll, but some—with your permission—take dogs to a park (see question 78). They operate differently in compact cities than they do in more spread-out towns or suburbs. Dog walkers in Manhattan, for example, stroll from building to building to pick up and drop off dogs. Here in Tucson they have to drive to collect their walkees, so the number of dogs is limited by the size of the vehicle—and the ability of the dog walker to keep them calm while in transit.

In Manhattan, prices for dog walking might range from $14 per dog for a quick 15-minute piddle to $28 for one hour of exercise; in Tucson, on average, it's $25 for 40 minutes for up to two dogs in the same family; shorter stints are rare.

Some things to think about when considering a dog walker:

Affinity for the work

Does this person seem to like dogs in general and yours in particular, or do you get the sense she's just looking to make a quick buck with clients who can't tattle if she goofs off? In turn, does your usually friendly dog cozy up to her—or slink off? Dogs are generally excellent judges of character.

Credentials

American Red Cross Certification in pet first aid and CPR are definite pluses, as is membership in a professional pet sitter's organization. Having training credentials (see Chapter 6) is also an asset.

References

Although these are always important to check, it's particularly crucial for a person who will be entering your home. There's a certain irony to the fact that dog walkers are usually most popular in backyard-challenged urban areas, where trust is not at a premium. It's not unreasonable for you to ask where your dog walker lives to even the playing field. Or to mention that you know someone who's connected.

General philosophy and dog knowledge

Ask what your potential walker would do if your dog misbehaves. If he advocates an alpha roll—or a Tootsie Roll—reconsider.

Logistic specifics

Will your dog be staying on a leash the entire time? Will the route involve crossing lots of city streets or busy roads? How many other dogs will be coming along? What do you do with the rest of the group when you're picking a dog up at an apartment building?* The responses should help you figure out if your dog's personality and the dog walker's plans are in synch with each other, and if you feel comfortable about your dog's safety.

Formalities

A professional should have you fill out a form with your emergency numbers (including that of your vet); provide you with his emergency contact information; ask you to confirm in writing that your dog has had all the required shots and identification/registration (in case she's an escape artist), and has no history of serious aggression; and provide you with a contract that specifies which services will be rendered and when—and how much you'll pay for them.

Before you sign on, go for a test walk (with payment of course): just you, your dog, and the dog walker. See how your pup—and any poop she might produce—is handled. If your dog walker doesn't scoop, she's either not paying attention to your dog or she's a bad global citizen.

DAYCARE

Forget sterile rooms with cramped cages. Today's doggie day-care (a.k.a. doggie day camp) is likely to resemble nursery school more than it does a kennel, replete with organized play-, nap-, and snack periods and even webcams that let you see what your pup is up to. Organized activities often abound, with training filling in for coloring. Indeed, some doggie daycare centers outshine the kiddie versions; the latter are unlikely to have hairdressers or doctors on site.

In spite of all these extras, daycare might be more cost effective than a dog walking service. For one thing, you don't have

---

* As opposed to "I bundle the pack into the elevator," or "I leave them tied up outside, unattended," the correct answer is, "I have my super-reliable assistant wait with them."

to—in fact shouldn't—send your dog every day. Limiting day-care to two or three times a week keeps your dog from getting overstimulated and from considering the experience mundane. And rates are not generally outrageous. A spot check of upscale facilities around the country showed costs ranging from $25 for a half day for dogs weighing under 25 pounds in Scottsdale to $55 for a full day for plus size pups (more than 85 pounds) in Manhattan. Membership or monthly passes lower the rates even more.

How to find a good play center? The same way as you find dog walkers, many of whom may be affiliated with daycare centers. In some major metropolitan areas, daycare/boarding facilities are rated online, similar to hotels and restaurants.

You should also have the same concerns, from treatment philosophy to poop-scooping. Ask questions in advance, and then observe the proceedings without your dog. If possible, arrange to go in during a play period, so you can see how the group is handled.

The service contract that requires you to provide detailed information, including emergency contacts and authorization for emergency treatment, is even more crucial. Your dog, of course, has been neutered or spayed and has had all the required vaccinations, but if the center doesn't insist on verification, it means they're not confirming the data on all the other, less perfect, dogs.

Staff

Again, think dog walkers, multiplied: expect, at a minimum, to find people who like and know how to handle dogs. They should be able to gauge when dogs need a rest, and when they need to be separated from each other—and how to accomplish that. Knowledge of training is a bonus. If there's no vet on staff—some places have them—there should be one on call.

Staff quantity is also important. There shouldn't be more than 10 dogs per staff person (and more than 35 to 40 dogs, total, at a facility is pushing it).

Environment

Is there enough room—and is it well divided, so that dogs have separate areas for play and rest? If there are crates, are they large enough for comfort? Some people insist on no-crate facilities but if your dog is used to being crated, there's nothing wrong with providing him with an escape he's used to. That said, you'd want a doggie cam—or spot visit—to prove that your dog is not caged all day.

Do the floors have no-skid rubber surfaces? Concrete can be bad for footpads and painful for arthritic dogs or pups with hip problems.

Are nontoxic cleaners used? Of course you don't want a place to smell bad, but the (cleaning) solution can be worse than the problem. Chlorine bleach-based products produce toxic fumes when mixed with the ammonia in urine. A daycare should know the basics of pet chemistry; otherwise, who knows what else they don't know?

Is the daycare well ventilated and temperature controlled? Your dog should have plenty of air, and not be subjected to extremes of either heat or cold. If you wouldn't be comfortable there, your dog probably wouldn't be either.

If there's a yard that the dogs play in, is it secure? Can your escape artist manage to scale the fence or dig under it?

Interaction with other dogs

How often will the dogs be together? Too much playtime can be exhausting; too little may mean too little exercise. Are the activities organized or carefully supervised, or are there doggie free-for-alls? Are dogs grouped by size and activity level (hyper versus low key) when they play? Again, groups should be small enough to allow good staff supervision.

How does the staff handle introducing new dogs? You should expect your dog to be presented to each dog individually, rather than just being thrown into the pack. Are all collars removed? During rough play, dogs can get entangled, and I don't mean romantically. (Of course, romantic entanglement would be undesirable, too, which is why pups that are not spayed or neutered are banned from daycare.)

Amenities

Some places offer food (at an extra cost), but it's better to provide your own; dogs don't do well with diet changes. Still, if another dog steals your pooch's dinner, it's good to know he won't go hungry. As I noted before, some places offer everything from training to grooming. If the price is right—and the other dogs using the services look attractive and are polite—why not take advantage of these one-stop options?

NETWORKING

If you can't afford either dog walking or daycare—or prefer something less formal—consider arranging play dates or care exchanges through such online networks as dogster.com or pawspot.com.

It's like Internet dating, only with less stress about whether you'll be considered attractive and more concern about getting bitten (depending on the sites you ordinarily frequent, of course; you may be vampire oriented). Get to know the other owner in a public place and make sure your dogs get along before going to someone else's home or inviting someone into yours.

There are no guarantees, but there are none in professional care either. And it may be the start of a beautiful doggie friendship.

77. WHAT ORGANIZED ACTIVITIES ARE AVAILABLE FOR ME TO DO WITH MY DOG?

What activities *aren't* available is the better question. I was amazed—and exhausted just contemplating—how many things there are to do with dogs in a group, and how many titles you (collectively) can aspire to. Nor are the games just for purebreds, as they were in the past; many now have versions geared to the doggie hoi polloi. The only prerequisite: your dog has to be trained to follow instructions.

For the full range of possibilities, including carting, hunting, Schutzhund (which is as scary as it sounds), sheepherding, skijoring, tracking, and water sports (though not synchronized swimming), see DogPlay (www.dogplay.com). To find events in your area, check the American Kennel Club (AKC; www.akc.org) event search option or Google the name of your city and the activity you're interested in. Many pet stores post events, too.

The following are the five most popular sports and are open to the greatest number of dogs.

AGILITY

Started in the late 1970s in London, and modeled on horse show jumping, agility has come to mean many things to many dog people—all of whom agree it's a blast. Essentially, you direct your dog through an obstacle course—which almost always involves seesaws, tables, poles, tires, and lots of weaving around and jumping—and are judged on both time and accuracy.

COMPETITIVE OBEDIENCE

Sure your dog can sit and stay in the privacy of your own home, but can she—and you—perform under pressure? Various levels of command conformity range from the Novice Long Sit (no whining permitted) to Advanced Scent Discrimination, where your dog must identify leather and metal items that you've touched. Who knew there were arenas in which strong body odor was a plus?

CANINE FREESTYLE (A.K.A. MUSICAL FREESTYLE)

If Frankie was more coordinated,* this is the competition I'd most want to try. Nicknamed "dancing with dogs," it sets obedience to music, with routines that participants create. Costumes may or may not be part of the proceedings.

---

* *Okay, okay, this is a classic case of "blame the dog" when you fart. I can't afford to pay off everyone who knows the truth: Frankie has an adorable prancing gait, like a tiny Lipizzaner stallion, while I'm the big ol' klutz.*

FLYING DISC

You know your dog's a natural, so why just toss a Frisbee around the park when you can impress far more people with his prowess? Events include "toss and fetch" (a.k.a. "mini-distance" or "throw and catch"), a straightforward skill demonstration using a single disc; and "dynamic freestyle," the Cirque du Soleil of the sport, involving short routines to music with multiple discs. Expect lots of spinning, leaping, and other physical pyrotechnics.

FLYBALL

If both you and your dog play well with others, this relay-style agility competition with hurdles and tennis balls may be your sport. If no pooch misses a hurdle or drops a tennis ball, the team that completes the course with the fastest time wins.

Also popular with mixed breeds are Earthdog, which simulates tunneling for simulated rodents; Strong Dog, similar to Earthdog, but the faux rodents have to be brought back to the handler; and Lure Coursing, chasing something fast-moving across a real, not simulated, field. See the National All-Breed Sporting Association (NABSA; www.go-k9sport.org) for details on these games.

78. I'VE NEVER BEEN TO A DOG PARK. ARE THERE RULES?

Definitely; both stated and implicit. The former are usually posted and easy to follow (though not everyone does), but observing the latter is equally important if you want to fit in with the regulars. Dog parks are similar to playgrounds, with a bit more snarling and public peeing but no less snobbery and gossip.

First, a definition: A dog park—sometimes called a dog run—is an enclosed area set aside for dogs to play together off leash. Some are spacious enough to offer separate areas for big and small dogs; others are parking lot size. Some are verdant and lush; others have dirt for décor. Picnic benches and tables may be provided; sometimes it's BYO folding chairs. Water and baggies for cleanups are usually available.

Not all dogs (or owners) are good candidates for dog parks. Again, shyness and aggressiveness are equally problematic. I took Frankie to a dog park about a month after I got him, without any preparation or training. He spent the entire time trying to jump into my lap or attach himself to my leg.

Frankie never did warm up to the dog park, which probably had more to do with occurrences in his mysterious past than with my foolish full-immersion introduction to it. Still, if I had a do-over, I would have come to the park during off hours—very early or following the after-work rush—when fewer dogs were around, and try to ease him into a new and stressful situation.

No matter how friendly your dog, some training—at minimum, obedience to a recall—is essential. There are bound to be renegades—their owners would say free spirits—at any dog park, but it takes two to tangle. Before you go, observe and have your pup engage in play, so you get a sense of what falls within the realm of normal. As per Chapter 6, it's important to know the basics of Doglish, especially your pup's dialect, so you can read body language effectively.

Finally, on the first visit, quit while you're ahead, i.e., while your dog is enjoying herself. Stay no more than 15 or 20 minutes. Your dog will look forward to returning if she's tantalized, not overtired. And if she forgets all her training, and doesn't want to come to you when you're ready to go home, cut her some slack. This is a new experience, and if she doesn't want to leave, it's been a successful one.

When you go:

UNLEASH YOUR DOG AS SOON AS YOU'RE IN THE AREA WHERE IT'S PERMITTED, AND TAKE OFF HER COLLAR.

If your dog is tethered while others are running free, she'll be vulnerable, which is a prelude to a scuffle—as is the fact that she's likely to be protective of you if you're literally attached to her.

As I noted in the earlier daycare center section, collars can be dangerous during rough play. If you're in a secured area, there's no reason to leave one on. If you don't recognize your pup without his tags, you shouldn't be taking him out of the house.

DON'T BRING TREATS.

It's usually verboten, anyway, because all the dogs will sniff them out—and you don't want to be beset by the hungry hordes. And food is not only a source of dissent among canine contenders; bringing it will also annoy other owners whose dogs may be on a diet. If you do have treats and there's a particularly insistent pup, always ask the owner if it's okay to give her something. That'll go a long way toward smoothing any fur you've ruffled.

Water can be a source of strife, too, if it's not provided by the park. In that case, it may be a good idea to restrict drinking to before and after your park visit.

DON'T BRING TOYS THAT YOU DON'T WANT TO LOSE.

It's hard to keep track of pooch playthings under the best of circumstances, and with large numbers of dogs in motion ... forget it. You definitely don't want to bring along anything your dog is protective of and will fight to defend. Or that you'll fight to defend. Maybe it's a guy thing, but I've noticed that some men seem bound and determined to bring home *their* dog's tennis ball, no matter how old and dirty, rather than one belonging to someone else's pup.

BE VIGILANT BUT DON'T HOVER.

It's important to keep an eye on your dog while you're in the park, but there's no point bringing him there if you're not going to let him have fun. Helicopter owners annoy both dogs and humans.

TAKE RESPONSIBILITY FOR YOUR DOG'S BEHAVIOR.

If your dog is bullying other dogs, it's up to you to get him under control—and to not bring him back until he's learned better park manners (that doesn't include talking in his indoor voice; raucous barking is what dog parks are all about).

Ideally, you'll be aware when a fight is about to break out and command your dog to return to you and/or create a distraction. But if there is a fracas and it involves your charge, you— and the other owner—need to try to disentangle the dogs. Some possibilities for accomplishing that include making a loud noise such as clapping, throwing water at their heads, spraying them with citronella, or tossing a ball at their butts. For larger dogs, some experts suggest that each owner pull on the dog's back legs. Never grab a collar or otherwise put your hand near a dog's head; getting close to the teeth of an upset pup is a sure ticket to bite land.

The worst part of a dogfight may be the aftermath, when the humans get into the act. Try to stay calm, even—especially—if the fight was clearly the other dog's fault, and your dog is injured. Garnering sympathy for the plight of your poor pup, both on the part of the offending party and among witnesses, is more likely to get your vet bill paid than making yourself obnoxious. Don't forget to gather names and contact information.* In most cases, it's hard to assign blame, so drop the defensiveness, own up to your dog's role, and split any costs.

CLEAN UP AFTER YOUR DOG.

If I seem obsessed with feces, it's not because I'm a clean freak or a coprophiliac. It's just that we, the collective dog community, have to put our best feet forward because if other people put their feet forward into something stinky, they'll blame the dogs, and try to get dog-friendly facilities shut down.

---

* In fact, this is likely to be the first time you'll learn the other people's names. One of the implicit rules of the dog park is to avoid showing an untoward interest in the humans. You will be identified as, say, "Bella's mom" or "Hooter's dad." Of course, dog park romances do occur, in which case you will (probably) learn the other person's identity. Beware, however, of the dreaded dog park breakup if there are limited off-leash options in your town.

CHAPTER 8
FUN AND GAMES ON THE ROAD

79. I WANT TO GO ON VACATION WITH MY DOG. WHAT'S THE BEST MODE OF TRANSPORTATION?

RV or motor home. I never thought I'd write those words in a travel advice context, but if you're vacationing with family or friends, it's a great canine conveyance.

I saw the error of my snobbish ways when my friends Linda and Daniela bought an RV for their two-dog household. They came back from their first trip, to the California coast, raving about the experience.* They never had to worry about finding dog-friendly lodgings or coordinating bathroom and food stops for people and pooches.** And they always had easy access to hiking trails and other outdoorsy attractions. I'm not suggesting that you necessarily go out and invest in your own gas guzzler (Linda and Daniela are otherwise very green, honest), but depending on fuel prices and your city of residence, renting one might be cost effective as well as convenient.

Because buses and trains are not an option—except if you go with a charter; see the following question—your next best bet is car travel, which I'll discuss in question 80.

Planes? Unless you have a dog small enough to take into the cabin, don't mind traveling separately from your pup,† or can

---

* Well, except for the Deliverance-type guys at one campground, but they were exceptions. And my friends had Dasha and Madison, their two semi-large dogs, with them, looking semi-fierce.

** I was initially thinking that you could just pull over and have your dog go al fresco, but have since discovered Pup-Head Portable Potty with PupGrass, billed as "Ideal for Boats and RVs! Now your dog can relieve themselves [sic] when they're not able to get to 'real' grass."

† With Pet Airways (petairways.com), which debuted in 2009, your dog flies in the cabin—but not with you. It's a nice concept, but has several limitations, the least of which is the need to coordinate human and canine flights. In addition, only a few routes are currently available and certain breeds are excluded from air travel. (I think they'd behave better than drunk humans, but no one consulted me.)

afford a charter (see question 80), air travel is a bad idea. The pressure and temperature in the hold vary, making a noisy, noxious (think inhaling jet fuel fumes), and already terrifying experience even more terrifying and uncomfortable. And dogs can't even take chill pills. According to the American Veterinary Medical Association, sedatives and tranquilizers can create respiratory and cardiovascular problems at increased altitudes. They can also mess up your dog's equilibrium—which means she can't brace herself when her carrier is moved. And who wants a dizzy dog?

Even in the cabin, dogs with pushed-in faces, such as Pugs, are at an increased risk for breathing and heart problems. And because the carrier must fit under your seat—your dog won't be comfortable in the overhead baggage bins, the contents of which may shift—that limits the size of your accompanying dog. At 11 pounds and normally nosed, Frankie would be a good flight candidate but so far, I haven't attempted it; I'm afraid he would balk at removing his shoes and taking everything out of his pockets for the security check.

That said, I know a lot of people and small dogs who travel happily together. Indeed petite pups are such popular flight companions that JetBlue recently initiated a JetPaws program (www.jetblue.com/jetpaws), with, naturally, a line of jet-friendly accessories. Even if you're not on the airline's route, log on to the website for useful information on pet jetsetting, including the required documentation. Other airlines usually embed information on their carry-on canine policy some-where on their websites. Make sure you verify that policy, including all fees (JetBlue, for example, charges $100 each way per doggy passenger) by phone well in advance of your flight and before you make a reservation.

Only one cruise line, Cunard, allows dogs on board, and then only for transatlantic crossings on the flagship *Queen Mary 2.*

There are a limited number of kennel slots, and getting your dog's documents approved takes months of advance planning. All in all, canine cruising is only for those who have lots of time and money. But if you fall into that category, why not take your dog to the continent for the grand Smells of Europe tour?

80. IS THERE SUCH A THING AS A DOG TRAVEL AGENT?

Not really (although some Border Collies I know could probably organize trips for themselves and their people). Most of the companies that assist with travel arrangements are geared toward relocations rather than vacations. The closest you'll come is the Dogtravel Company (www.dogtravelcompany. net), which is not a travel agency but a members club for the pup obsessed. The annual membership fee is inexpensive but travel can be pricy because the trains and planes used are all chartered. Still, if you choose a popular route or can gather together a large group, it might not cost all that much to have your Great Dane sitting next to you in the cabin (though I can't say what kind of leg room you'll have).

That's not to suggest you won't find plenty of guidance for dog-centric travel. DogFriendly.com (the most comprehensive, with its own line of guides), BringFido.com (the best looking and easiest to navigate but with limited lodging information), and petswelcome.com (in between the two for appearance and utility, but with a good selection of off-beat lodgings) are among the increasing crop of websites that offer destination advice and travel tips along with booking engines for hotels.

81. WHAT DO I NEED TO KNOW ABOUT CAR TRAVEL WITH MY DOG?

Sometimes politicians can be instructive, if only by providing negative examples. You should not, for example, emulate presidential candidate Mitt Romney, who put the family dog, Seamus, into a crate, strapped him to the roof of the station wagon, and drove 12 hours from Boston to Ontario. Romney cited as an example of "emotion-free crisis management" having to hose the excrement produced by the traumatized Seamus off the car's roof and windows. I suspect this didn't win him any votes from animal lovers.

Nor, on the other end of the spectrum, should you applaud California governor Arnold Schwarzenegger, who vetoed a law that would have imposed a fine for driving with a dog in your lap. I have a personal stake in that misguided decision. When I visit my friend Clare in Santa Barbara, her dog, Archie, lounges politely in the back until we approach the beach—at which point he leaps into Clare's lap and squirms excitedly. Archie is a compact guy, but he's large enough to obstruct Clare's vision when he sits upright. Clare won't listen to me or to her other terrified passengers but—being a lawyer and therefore an officer of the court, as well as an upstanding citizen—she would obey the law if it existed.

ADDITIONAL SAFETY TIPS

Here are some additional safety tips you'll want to keep in mind when traveling.

Use restraint(s).

Buckle up for safety, both yours and your pup's. To those who argue that they don't want to restrict their dogs' freedom, I ask, "Would you want him to enjoy the freedom of going through the windshield?" An unrestrained dog can become a projectile if you have to stop short.*

And just because your unsecured dog is out of projectile range of your windshield, that doesn't mean she's safe from injury. It's very dangerous to let a dog ride in the open bed of a pickup truck. Approximately 100,000 dogs die every year from falling or jumping out of pickups and countless more are injured.

And untethered dogs pose not only safety issues but legal and economic ones. Many states have passed variations of the law in Washington, where it's a misdemeanor to "willfully transport or confine ... any domestic animal ... in a manner, posture or confinement that will jeopardize the safety of the animal or the public." (Some laws specify that this includes having a dog in the back of a pickup truck.) Accordingly, if your unsecured dog causes an accident, your insurance is rendered invalid under many policies. And even if the

---

* *Dogs have also been known to shift gears—and even take their owner's car for a short spin. To cite only a couple of recent examples, a Pit Bull left in a vehicle going through an automatic carwash in Pryor, Oklahoma, reversed it into traffic; and a Boxer/Shar-Pei mix drove his owner's idling van into a Long Island, New York, coffee shop. Neither dogs nor humans were injured in these incidents, but the Oklahoma owner had his license revoked—not because his dog was driving but because the police discovered that neither he (nor the Pit Bull) had auto insurance.*

accident is the other driver's fault, your vet bills won't be paid if your dog wasn't properly restrained.*

You'll achieve the best dog security with a harness—never, ever, a collar—hooked to the car's back seat belt. A regular harness will work in a pinch—pinch being the operative word—but the ones designed especially for travel have padding that insulates your dog against pressure caused by a sudden stop. The top models also have hooking mechanisms that let your dog move—though not too much—and are easy to click open and shut. See the "Product Reviews" section of AgilePooch.com for a travel halter comparison.

If your dog weighs fewer than 20 pounds, consider a booster seat, similar to the kiddie version. A pup that can gaze out the window is less likely to get bored or carsick (see the following).

Secured travel crates are another option, but even crate-trained dogs don't always respond well to being cooped up in a moving vehicle without being able to see where they're going. Some people use barriers that prevent their dogs from invading their personal driving space, but these are tough to fit all cars and all dogs; some pups manage to get past everything but steel. Nor do barriers prevent dangerous jostling; a high-speed collision could put your dog in jeopardy if he hits a heavy wall.

Don't leave your dog unattended inside the car when it's hot or cold outside.

The former is far more dangerous than the latter because cars (and dogs) heat up more quickly than they cool off: when

---

* You may also get a lot of unwelcome notoriety. While walking along the side of the road, author Stephen King was struck by a minivan. Driver Bryan Smith—who subsequently turned up as a character in one of King's books—claimed he had been distracted by his Rottweiler, who was moving around the vehicle, trying to raid the food cooler.

there's no breeze, it can take only a minute or so for a car to reach a fatal temperature, even if you crack open the window. Dogs don't have efficient self-cooling systems.

This sounds like a simple rule to observe—unless you're female and traveling solo. One summer, en route from Tucson to southern California, I needed to pee desperately. After driving for miles through the desert, I finally came to a gas station and convenience store. According to the big thermometer display, the mercury had hit 110°F.

I looked around outside. No bathrooms. Damn. They must be in the store. Hoping to pass him off as couture, I put Frankie into a tasteful leopard-print carrier and went in. We were stopped immediately by the clerk, who said that, because the store sold food, Frankie was a health violation. (Have you ever eaten a convenience store burrito? Now *there's* a health violation.) I explained that if I peed outside the front door it would also be a violation—one that the clerk would have to mop up. The crazy lady alert went off, and Frankie was permitted to stay with me. As I drove away relieved, I con- templated how unfair it is that women can't share the public urination experience with their dogs. I'm certain it's a source of man-and-dog bonding.

Don't drive with your dog's head out the window.

I know it looks cute, especially if you have a dog with ears that flop in the breeze. But flying objects and idiot drivers who pass too close can pose dangers; so can soot and smaller particles that may fly into your dog's eyes and ears. Leave the windows open wide enough for your dog to have air so he can sniff to his heart's content—but not enough to get his head through.

ADDITIONAL COMFORT TIPS

Comfort is the key to keeping a traveling dog happy.

Don't let sleeping dogs lie.

Your dog may be snoozing comfortably—and then wake up and decide she has to make a pit stop at an inconvenient time. Stop every few hours to let your dog stretch her legs and conduct her business. As with humans, hydration and healthy snacks are a good idea, too. Skip the squeaky toys, though. They can drive you to distraction.

Nix the nausea.

Sure, many dogs are eager to hit the road as soon as they hear the sound of rattling car keys, but as many as one in four experience car discomfort because of fear or inner ear imbalance. Frankie (naturally) falls into the first category: he shakes, salivates, and stands upright in his harness for hours, on red alert, if he's not sedated. I tried everything: taking him on short trips to nice places (as opposed to the vet); keeping the window open rather than using the A/C; buying a booster seat so he could look out; even playing soothing music (which I hated, so maybe he picked up the bad vibes). His comparative serenity in the midsize car I rented when my Hyundai was in the shop made me wonder if Frankie just needs a smoother ride, but I draw the line at buying an Escalade for him.*

And I'm lucky. Frankie doesn't throw up out of nervousness, as some dogs do. The lingering smell of dog vomit in the backseat can really put a crimp in a vacation.

But don't let motion commotion make you abandon the idea of traveling with your dog. You just have to find out what works for her—beforehand. In particular, experiment with

---

* *Of course, I got the Hyundai before I got Frankie. Who knows what I might do if this book becomes a best-seller and I can afford to upgrade my wheels? According to a study by the American Kennel Club, some 47 percent of dog owners take their pooches into account when buying an automobile. See the reviews on dogcars.com if you're among them.*

rations. One recommendation is to feed your dog less than half of what you normally would, and not immediately before you leave. Snacks along the road should suffice until you reach your destination.

Some puppies outgrow carsickness. Some respond to desensitization programs. For others, it's as simple as better temperature control, raising your dog so she can look out, or keeping her from looking out. That's what I mean. Because your dog can't tell you precisely what's causing the problem, you need to try all kinds of different solutions.

That's especially true with meds. Some people swear by botanicals like Rescue Remedy, and my friend Clare says that lavender oil—but only the pure variety—calms her Archie successfully. Neither did a thing for Frankie. The vet suggested azepromine (Ace), but I discovered that it just masks the symptoms, leaving your dog still fearful but immobilized. Dramamine didn't work at the vet's recommended dosage; neither did Benadryl. I had the best results, finally, with Valium, although it initially turned Frankie into a little love machine. He licked my face with great abandon before settling in to enjoy—well, not hate—the ride.

Cerenia, a drug developed expressly to prevent vomiting in dogs, was approved by the FDA in 2007. It's expensive, and the jury is still out on whether it's effective and/or has side effects. Do some research if you decide to try it.

82. WHAT SHOULD I BRING ALONG ON A VACATION WITH MY DOG?

Airline baggage restrictions—and surcharges—are more reasons for you to travel by car. If you've got limited trunk space, you can even strap stuff on the roof (except for your dog; see previous question).

You'll have two prime goals in packing: to replicate the comforts of home for your dog, and to keep her from getting lost and/or in trouble. A secondary goal is to avoid losing any security deposit you might have put down for a hotel room.

To those ends, bring the following items along on your trip.

NOURISHMENT

If you don't think you can find it on the road or in your destination, pack the same brand of food your dog normally eats, including his favorite treats. This will not only help provide a sense of continuity but prevent stomach upset. Assuming you don't want to carry containers with your local tap water, take or buy bottled water. Your dog may be used to the specific mix of noxious chemicals that your city's water supply provides and react badly to new ones.

Don't forget food and water bowls if you're not going to a hotel that provides them. You don't have to schlep your dog's personal raku bowl, unless he's really spoiled and refuses to eat from any other. For the nonpicky pup, easy-to-tote travel substitutes are fine.

SHELTER AND REST

This is one reason crate training is so useful: some hotels won't allow your dog to be left alone in a room if he's not crated—which creates problems if, say, you want to go out to dinner and your hotel doesn't have a pet sitting service (or if you don't want to shell out the extra money for one). A dog that loves his faux den will be happy to have a safe retreat in unfamiliar surroundings. If his usual crate isn't easily transportable, get your dog accustomed to a travel crate before you go.

Many upscale hotels provide pet beds, some of which are pretty darn cute (and are—surprise, surprise—for sale). I have never seen one yet, however, that Frankie was interested in, unless I placed it next to me on my bed, which pretty much defeats the hotel's purpose, i.e., to exile your dog to the floor. But again, it's a question of personal canine preference. You might need to take your dog's bed along as a security blanket— or simply allow him to hog your actual blanket, just like he does at home.

ENTERTAINMENT

Make sure to take along some of your dog's favorite playthings—especially chew toys, if you need to divert her from the hotel's yummy furniture. But don't include anything that's impossible to replace; things may get pushed under the bed and left behind. Again, I speak from experience. I've discovered that the hotel staff doesn't tend to dispatch drooly objects to lost-and-found for guest retrieval.

CLEANER-UPPERS

Here's the part where wanting not to pay a security deposit or offend your hosts, even if they're family, come in. Bring along old towels to wipe your pup's paws when you come in from outdoors, and some old sheets to put down on the furniture in case your dog likes to lounge on it, shedding happily and obliviously.

I'm not sure how many people take their dogs with them on business trips—at least on business trips that require them to look spiffy—but if you're among them, don't forget your lint and hair remover.

Finally, I don't have to tell you again to take along bags to collect your pooch's poop, do I?

HEALTH AND EMERGENCIES

Be sure you've got any medications your dog needs, or may need—and a cooler to keep them in, in case your hotel doesn't come equipped with a fridge.*

If you live with a large escape artist, this might be the time to consider a GPS collar (they're usually too heavy for small dogs, who are easier to keep hold of in any case). Even mellow dogs run off at rest stops—whether out of the fear that you're driving them to a new home, or a sense of adventure, or ... who knows? At the least, make sure your dog is wearing a collar with your cell phone information on it. Affixing a tag with your destination data couldn't hurt either. Sometimes dogs manage to slip their collars, so before you leave, be sure to update your dog's microchip with your current contact information and any health issues you need the person who locates him to be aware of (in my case, Frankie's diabetes).

That first aid kit that's been gathering dust in your dog's toy chest? Take it along. You never know. That's true of shot certifications, too. If your normally calm pup takes a skin-breaking nip out of someone, you want everyone to know his rabies shots are up to date. Hotels that have pet care facilities may require proof of vaccination(s) in any case.

83. WHICH LODGINGS ARE LIKELY TO WELCOME MY DOG (AND ME)?

The hospitality industry has discovered that being dog friendly is smart business. Canine acceptance has become common, in spite—or, perhaps, because—of the economic downturn. It makes sense to do whatever you can to fill beds, even if it means filling them with furry bodies.

---

* And in case you don't want to open the minibar, lest its oversensitive sensors charge you for a bottle of something expensive that you didn't actually drink. Yes, I speak from experience.

As a result, you've got a vast number of choices of places to stay, from posh resorts with exclusive dog amenities to rustic, activity-oriented camps devoted entirely to pooches and their people. I've broken them down into some basic categories, outlining what you can expect when you stay there. In all cases, be sure to check and recheck the pet policies when you make reservations, and confirm that your dog fits the size/ weight limits.

UTILITARIAN

Many standard motel chains—among them, Best Western, Comfort Inn, La Quinta, Holiday Inn, Inn and Out Burgers,* Motel 6, Quality Inn, Residence Inn, Red Roof Inn—allow guests to bring at least one "well-behaved family pet" (as opposed to one ill-tempered circus lion?). Charges vary from the vague "liable for any damages" to nonrefundable fees that run as high as $100 per stay.

---

* I just wanted to see if you were paying attention. But that would be a great name for a dog motel with a limited room service menu, wouldn't it? Consider it copyrighted.

Some motels put a limit on the size and number of dogs you can bring in; many do not. Among the odder formulations I came across is one that states, "Dogs up to 75 pounds are allowed for an additional one time pet fee of $75 per room. There may be one dog up to 75 pounds or two dogs that total 75 pounds per room." Anyone who thinks that one laid back English Mastiff will cause more ruckus than two Jack Russell Terriers, doesn't know, well, jack about dogs.

As you might imagine, no special amenities are offered in dog-friendly motel chains. If you're lucky, you won't get stuck in a smoking room. I understand that cleaning and allergies are an issue, but (most) dogs don't stink nearly as much as stale cigarettes.

You're required to note the presence of your dogs on the on-line reservation forms. However, I suspect that some motel desk clerks wouldn't know or care if you brought in a menagerie, including that circus lion, if you turn up off-season and lots of rooms are available. One summer Clare and I and Frankie and Archie needed a place to stay in Palm Springs.* The clerk at the Motel 6 we found seemed bored when I mentioned that we had two small dogs with us—and probably would have been equally uninterested if I had said "two small male hookers."

RUSTIC/NATURAL

Those who literally want to sleep in a pup tent—and don't underestimate a dog's body heat, for better and for worse—have a lot of options open to them. Many campgrounds are dog friendly, with special dedicated pet areas, suggested hiking trails, and so on.

---

* This was because, after our first two nights there, the wonderful Polynesian-themed Caliente Tropics motel had been entirely booked with a tiki-lovers conference. Who knew there was so much tiki culture to celebrate beyond umbrella drinks?

Cabins and cottages are an excellent alternative for those who, as I do, prefer a firmer barrier between themselves and the great outdoors. Indoor bathrooms put me in a far better state of mind for appreciating nature—which remains easily accessible to Frankie. Some of these lodgings are pretty upscale. Frankie and I particularly enjoyed the luxe cottages at L'Auberge de Sedona, set in a lovely wooded area of Sedona with the proverbial burbling creek.

HOMEY

Frankie doesn't like to interact with strangers first thing in the morning and, being diabetic, can't take advantage of the lavish morning meals that are part of the bed and breakfast experience. He also worries about getting a dewclaw caught on a lace antimacassar. But Frankie has a tendency toward stereotyping. The B&Bs that accept dogs are not usually of the frou-frou variety and are often in beautiful settings. And you can expect a lot of personalized advice about local pup-friendly places.

LUXE

This is the category I know best—not because I was ever rich but because, as a travel writer, I got comped at some pretty hoo-hah places, and Frankie happily freeloaded whenever he could. Most of the hotels and resorts we visited were within easy driving distance of Tucson because I was researching *Arizona for Dummies,* but we ventured as far as California to meet Clare and Archie, and were treated like celebrities at Le Merigot in Santa Monica (great beach location and excellent gift bags—just what you would expect from a hotel near Hollywood).

With Frankie weighing in at a svelte 11 pounds, he and I were able to stay at many places that limit their pups to 20 (sometimes 25) pounds or less.* However, a number of upscale chains, including Loews, Kimpton, and Sofitel are not sizeist (if your dog weighs fewer than 80 pounds you're okay at Sheratons, too). Most require nonrefundable deposits or daily "cleaning" fees, some quite hefty. You will also have to sign a liability form, promising—well, lots of things, such as never to leave your dog alone in the room and never to let her use the hotel pool (even though dogs are far less likely than children to pee in the water).**

In addition to dog walking and sitting services (for an extra fee, naturally), some of the perks you're likely to encounter at high-end resorts and hotels include ...

Information

You can almost certainly depend on getting a packet detailing local dog facilities, from maps to nearby parks to lists of veterinarians and dog-friendly restaurants. Sometimes you'll also encounter a pet concierge—human or canine. Consider, for example, Luke, the rescued Yellow Lab who holds that position at the Fairmont San Antonio. He isn't very good at restaurant recommendations—he thinks dogs should be able to eat everywhere and sample everything on the menu—but he provides a friendly doggy welcome to all members of his species and their humans who check into his hotel.

---

* Don't worry if you're in the general ballpark, size-wise; no one will humiliate you by weighing your dog. Archie, who is 28 pounds—all muscle, but a bit taller than Frankie—had no problem passing muster when Clare and I checked him into an Arizona resort that had a 25-pound limit.

** However, the James Chicago Hotel offers an indoor saltwater lap pool built especially for dogs, with skinny-dipping permitted (perhaps even required).

Amenities

As I mentioned earlier, you'll often find a dog bed (everything from a large pillow to the snug form-fitting kind) in your hotel room. Dog bowls and mats are usually provided, too. The beds are generally yours for a price; the bowls may or may not be intended for transport; and anything personalized—usually just mats—is unambiguously yours. When in doubt, ask, lest you find a surprise on your credit card tab.

Always yours to take home are the goodie bags you're likely to receive. Frankie has been gifted with everything from a dog-sized backpack—replete with foldable bowls for the hiking trail (Frankie said no thanks, I'm not a Sherpa)—and squeaky toys to a DVD of *My Dog Skip*. Biscuits from a local dog bakery are frequently included* and, almost invariably, small plastic bags. I'm happy to have them; I just don't like the fact that these not-so-subtle hints that you're expected to clean up after your pup are labeled luxury amenities.** Moreover, sometimes they're pink and scented, which doubly offends me, because Frankie is male and his poop doesn't stink.

Room service

Various combinations of meat, fish, brown rice, eggs, and veggies labeled with clever, dog-related names are often available to be delivered to your door. Usually the meat is ground beef or grilled chicken, but some places, such as the Peninsula Beverly Hills, highlight such items as "Spot's New York Strip, a juicy 8 oz. grilled steak served sliced and garnished with baby carrots ($19)." I have been known to order food

---

* *One Arizona resort that only accepts dogs who weigh less than 20 pounds presented Frankie with a welcome biscuit that was bigger than his head. If he had managed to get hold of, and consume, the entire thing, I would have had to pay for vomit cleanup.*

** *I received an item with the unfortunate name of "Bon Ton Luxury Pet Disposal Kit," which sounds like something Tony Soprano might have used to dispatch an irritating Shih Tzu.*

"for Frankie" and eat most of it. Hey, Frankie can't down a half-pound steak, and I'm not going to find one on a human room service menu for less than 20 bucks.

Some hotels also offer "premium" brand dog foods that would never pass Frankie's lips. I suggest you BYOK (bring your own kibble) if your pooch is accustomed to dining on pellets.

Activities

Just because your dog is on vacation doesn't mean she can't get an education. At the Mandarin Oriental in Miami, for example, you can get a certified dog trainer to work with you (and your dog) on correcting behavior issues. Group classes are also offered at several places.

Want to mingle with other dogs and their traveling companions? Yappy hours such as the one at the Hotel Monaco Alexandra let pups and their people meet and greet with species-appropriate beverages and snacks.

Spa/grooming services

Not only are many hotels teaming up with grooming businesses for pup primping; some even offer in-room* spa services such as massages.

Frankie was treated to a massage at the Sheraton Wild Horse Pass Resort near Phoenix. He initially went along with the program, albeit reluctantly, allowing his little limbs to be stretched and his flank to be kneaded, but he refused to turn over to let the massage therapist work on the other side. I don't think he's likely to recommend the treatment to his pup pals.

---

* Oddly, some humans don't want to share the actual spa with dogs.

Assorted

My two favorite perks don't involve pampering, just simple but inspired concepts. At the Kimpton Hotels—the one I visited was FireSky in Scottsdale—your dog's name is posted on a chalkboard at the property entryway. Imagine how proud Frankie felt to see his name prominently displayed every time we came in!

And if you check into the Fairmont Washington, D.C., with a dog (or, to be fair, a cat), the hotel will donate 5 percent of the room rate to the Washington Animal Rescue League. It's too bad only dogs smaller than 20 pounds are permitted, thus limiting the largesse, but it's still a terrific reminder that dogs don't need massages and pedicures; they just need a good home.

ALL DOG, ALL THE TIME

Want to optimize the time spent with your dog and vacation with other people who are equally canine crazy? Consider a retreat where dog attendance is obligatory. These getaways, with names such as Camp Gone to the Dogs, Paws and Pals, Camp Barking Hills, or Camp Winnaribbun, may offer dorm rooms or rustic cabins where both you and your dog bunk; in some cases, nearby accommodations are arranged. Activities might include agility trials, swimming lessons, lectures on dog communication ... even instructions in dog-hair spinning. Typically, these camps are limited—perhaps two weeklong sessions a year or selected weekends. For a full listing with details, see www.dogplay.com/Activities/camps.html.

Note: Not all dogs are happy campers. Think carefully about whether your dog would be well-suited for a lot of social activity.

84. WHERE'S THE BEST PLACE TO LEAVE MY DOG IF I CAN'T TAKE HIM WITH ME?

If you have family or friends who are willing to take your dog in, and a dog who's willing to stay with them, you've got it made. Not only do you get free dogsitting, but anyone who agrees to care for your pup is probably close enough to you (or owes you enough) to put up with you calling several times a day and asking to put your pooch on the phone. Don't forget to bring back gifts for the caretakers as well as for your dog.

Similarly, if you've successfully arranged play dates through dog networks, a longer vacation exchange might be worth trying. And most doggie daycare centers offer overnight boarding. See question 76 for details about both.

But there are dogs—and, yes, I'm talking about Frankie again—who don't like to leave home. They're stressed enough that you're going away; mess with their lives any more and they're over the top. This is where dogsitters come in.

You'll find them the same way as you'll find doggie daycare centers and dog walkers: referrals from friends, dog park acquaintances, vets, organizations such as The Pet Sitting Directory (www.petsittingdirectory.com) or the National Association of Professional Pet Sitters (www.petsitters.org), and ... well, you never know. I found one great dogsitter through a local chef that I'm friendly with. He'd asked me where I'd been traveling lately, and when I told him I hadn't really gone anywhere since Frankie was diagnosed with diabetes, he suggested I try Linda, his former pastry chef, who had started a dog-sitting business. I tend to trust people who know how to make desserts (and are insured and bonded). Sure enough, Linda was terrific with Frankie and his shots.

When Linda wasn't available, I called my vet's office and discovered that Sarah, one of the receptionists, had just started a
dog-sitting business. Frankie was fond of her, and Sarah had
the three vets in the practice on speed dial. What more could
you ask for? Oh yes, communication: both Linda and Sarah
e-mailed me with a Frankie status report at least once a day,
often more.

In a typical arrangement, the dogsitter will stay overnight and
feed and walk your dog in the morning and evening. Unless
you pay extra for the sitter to check in, your dog is generally
on her own during the day. Again, fees range by location—
and expertise. I used to pay $25 for a college student to hang
out with Frankie but when insulin shots got involved, the
rates rose (I've paid from $40 to $65). Expect prices to go
up commensurately in major metropolitan areas, but resist
offers to exchange a stay in your conveniently located Manhattan or San Francisco apartment for free dog care—unless,
of course, the offerer falls into the trusted family or friends
category. Your pup might not get the attention she deserves
from a sitter looking to enjoy a slice of big city life.

CHAPTER 9
BETTER DOG HOMES AND GARDENS

85. IS IT OKAY TO LEAVE MY DOG OUTDOORS WHEN I'M NOT HOME?

If you don't live in an apartment building;* if you have a secure yard; if the weather isn't too hot or too cold; and if your dog has a shelter to duck into—maybe. But you need to consider other, less predictable, factors. For example, in the desert Southwest, it wouldn't be wise to leave a small dog vulnerable all day to attack by a territorial bird of prey.**

A day outdoors should provide fresh air, visual stimulation, and unlimited bathroom access for your dog. It should not be designed to keep him from destroying the house—that's what training and the suggestions in the following question are for—or as a form of punishment. Nor should the outdoors be

---

*   *I may have sacrificed easy access to art cinemas by moving from Manhattan to Tucson, but I never have to leave home when Frankie needs to heed nature's call (and Frankie never has to be subjected to doggie diapers while he's still continent). I'm not sure if it's a good or bad sign that I now consider this a reasonable tradeoff.*

** *I'm thinking of the Cooper's Hawk that sometimes swoops into my backyard for a small-bird snack and wouldn't appreciate Frankie's continuous presence. I concede that, in Manhattan, pigeons may be annoying but they generally observe a beaks-off canine policy.*

associated with social isolation. If you don't have a dog door, let your pup in the house as soon as you come home—or, at least, right after you go to the bathroom. (Dogs either stare at you with intense interest while you go, or hold vigil outside if you close the door to what they clearly believe is a teletransporter, hurtling you to another dimension.)

The following are some preconditions for better outdoor dog living.

SECURE YARD

By this I mean a yard that has a barrier that can't be breached by other animals (including humans)—generally, a fence with a locked gate. Opacity is desirable, too. An attractive dog like Frankie might prove extremely tempting to thieves, for example, while large, scary looking breeds inspire some macho idiots—you know, the ones who tease tigers in the zoo—to annoy these captive pups.

Decidedly not included in the secure category—by virtue of both visibility and of cruelty—is a yard guarded by an electric fence. Electric fences leave your dog open to outside harassment, including by malevolent squirrels, who can scamper in and out at will. These fences are also counterproductive. If your dog runs away—and why wouldn't he want to?—it's unlikely he would want to risk another shock by coming back in. (Yes, electric fence varieties exist that give your dog a "correction" until he returns to the perimeter—but that doesn't resolve such issues as squirrel harassment.)

On the other end of the security spectrum are tall masonry or brick walls—a dream for keeping your dog safe while he plays outdoors. Zoning and economics might dictate your use of other materials to build a barrier, however, as might your dog's natural drives. Consider the following behaviors when deciding on exactly how to secure your yard.

Chewing

An oral fixation could rule out wooden fencing; many dogs find tree-based products very tasty. You don't want your pooch to chew through slats and get a mouthful of splinters. The good news: dogs often outgrow an inclination toward dental entertainment, and you may eventually be able to install more attractive fencing.

Digging

I'll go into more detail about digging in question 89, but if you live with a serious burrower, fortify the fence line with cement blocks or large rocks, or dig a narrow trench and fill it with concrete. Alternatively, sink chicken wire into the ground about 6 to 12 inches deep, curving it in 2 or 3 feet toward the yard. Make sure to roll up the sharp edges so your dog doesn't injure herself.

Leaping

For the garden variety, as it were, fence jumper, regular precautions might suffice. Avoid leaving anything near the fence that your dog could use as a launch pad—patio table, garbage can, barbecue ... even piles of snow could give your pup an extra leg up. For Olympic-level vaulters, add height to the fence and tilt it inward with angled steel extensions, perhaps strung with fence fabric (but nothing that could trap your dog's paw or collar).

Another option is to plant shrubbery—or install a barrier that your dog can't impale himself on—at a distance designed to thwart a running start.

Note: If it's too expensive for you to go the whole fence route and/or your dog is a serious escape artist, consider a smaller—but large enough to roam in and use as a bathroom—enclosure, built adjacent to the house and in conjunction with a dog door (see the following section).

GIVE THEM SHELTER

Doghouses were once modest structures, intended only for basic protection against the elements—thus their reputation as retreats of last resort for the human badly behaved. Now they've gone from crude shelter to shelter magazine. Some architects advertise their design skills with elaborate dog homes; magazines from *This Old House* to *Woman's Day* have featured canine-sized renditions of classic American styles.

Can't afford a custom-built replica of your abode? No worries. You can still cater to your dog's comfort and your aesthetic sense with (theoretically) easy-to-construct models. Styles listed on DogHouse.com, for example, range from the Arctic-themed Dogloo ($120) to the porch-fronted Swiss chalet ($387)—not to mention the 8-foot-tall Victorian-style cottage that doubles as a kennel ($5,800).

Consider the following when buying a doghouse.

Size

Get a house large enough for your dog to fit his entire body into, but not so large as to be drafty. (If your pup is a social animal, you can get a duplex.) DogHouse.com offers tips on how to choose the correct size—for example, the door height opening should be no less than three fourths of the dog's shoulder-to-ground measurement.

Suitability

Plastic and wood are the most common doghouse materials; metal may be an option, too. Take the weather conditions in your region into account when you decide which to choose. Wood is probably a bad idea in a wet or snow-bound area, for example, although a pitched roof can help offset precipitation issues.

Placement

Again, consider geography. If you live in the Midwest, say, you don't want the opening of the doghouse to face the wind during the coldest time of year. In the Southwest, you need to avoid the midday sun in summer.

Insulation/protection

You may not have the wherewithal to install central heating or A/C in your dog's daytime quarters, but insulation is essential where temperatures are extreme.* Some pricey models have built-in protection, and off-center doors help keep the wind and rain from reaching your pup. Hanging strips of plastic over the doghouse door also helps ward off the elements, and putting a blanket, heated pad, or even straw on the floor keeps your dog toasty.

Amenities

Especially if he doesn't have access to your house while you're gone, your pup needs a supply of fresh water in his doghouse. Nix the food, however, except in toys that make it difficult to get to. Comestibles—remember Chapter 4?—may attract the bad company noted in the next section.

Cleanliness

No, a doghouse doesn't have to pass the white glove test, but you'd be surprised at the company your dog may be keeping if you're not vigilant: pack rats, bees, and other undesirables. Plastic houses are generally the easiest to clean, but some

---

* Leaving your dog inside under those circumstances is a far better idea, but sometimes temperatures fluctuate unexpectedly. And northern breeds may nag you to let them stay outside and play in the snow.

wood ones come with removable roofs. Consider, too, a raised panel floor: it keeps the air flowing and the debris under the house, not in it.

ENTRY AND EXIT STRATEGIES

Call it providence or serendipity. Before I got Frankie, I bought a home that caters to a small dog's comings and goings.* The sliding-glass doors on the side of my house are fronted by wrought-iron security bars that are a Frankie-size distance from one another. Tucson's warm weather and general non-bugginess allows me to leave the glass doors open without a screen much of the year; when I'm home, Frankie can exit and reenter without asking permission.

Installing a dog door typically requires you to cut a hole in a standard door or wall. Most door models come in three standard sizes, and of course you can pay extra to get something tailored to your pup's proportions. The larger the door, the more of a temperature control and security issue** it poses.

Perhaps the biggest decision you'll need to make regards the operation of the door: manual or automatic/electronic.

Manual

Generally consisting of flaps that your dog can walk through at will, manual doors used to be simple and inexpensive but

---

* Other animals enter only occasionally, no doubt aware of the fierce dog guarding the premises (the fence around my backyard helps, too). When Frankie first came to live with me, however, a large neighborhood cat decided to check him out. I spotted Frankie walking backward through the dining room into the kitchen, keeping a careful eye on the kitty while trying to elude her. Perhaps it was shame over this early incident that has made him such a vigilant home protector ever since.

** You might think that a large dog door would signal the presence of a large dog and thus deter robbers, but that's not always the case, as a homeowner in Shawnee, Kansas, discovered. According to a local news report, after noticing several missing items, Paul Vanlerberg set up a surveillance camera. The video it produced showed that the thieves crawled in through the dog door and helped themselves to liquor, cash, and electronics without rousing the door's intended user. Bad dog!

neither weather-tight nor secure. Many newer models, however, remain economical but provide better protection against both the elements and uninvited visitors. Some, for example, have a space between the two flaps that insulates against the weather. Others offer a simple locking mechanism such as a slide-in plastic panel that allows you to secure the door whenever you like.

Automatic/electronic*

The premise is the same for all varieties: your dog wears a special collar that allows him—and only him, as opposed to the random raccoon—to unlock the door, which then shuts behind him automatically. These doors vary in the type of technology they employ—from magnetic to battery-powered infrared and radio-frequency—as well as in style. Some resemble traditional flap doors; others glide up and down.

I applaud the dog empowerment concept and the added security these doors afford but they're costly to install and repair. And I don't entirely trust the technology. I once put in a battery-operated doorbell that went off constantly and indiscriminately, generally in the middle of the night, whenever ... well, I'm not sure what set the bell off—police radar? Garage door openers? When it comes to a door dropping down on your dog or locking him out of the house, we're talking about more than just an annoyance.

86. DOES MY HOUSE HAVE TO GO TO THE DOGS, OR ARE THERE WAYS TO KEEP IT LOOKING NICE?

Loving your dog and wanting lovely digs are by no means mutually exclusive. It's often just a question of stepping up

---

* According to pet-supplies-review.com, an "electronic" door usually refers to one that unlocks a flap that your dog may then push open, while "automatic" means a door that swings or slides open itself when your dog approaches.

the training and making a few inexpensive décor changes. But if you want to redecorate with your pup in mind, you don't have to sacrifice style to avoid permanent slobber stains.

Note: Dogs are notoriously bad at wiping their feet when they enter the house. Keep an old towel by the door and head your dog off at the pass before she has a chance to bring the outdoors in—in a bad way.

FLOORING

Tile is a no-brainer for the canine inclined, the harder and the more impervious to scratches the better; unlike carpeting, tile repels hair and odors, and is simple to clean. Wood floors are also dog-durable, although larger pooches can scratch the softer varieties; these may require a factory finish laminate— and a strict nail-trimming regimen—to maintain their good looks. Linoleum, which is tough, inexpensive, and environment friendly,* has made a comeback, so don't rule it out because you're picturing the colors and patterns of an ancient relative's kitchen.

Because much of this flooring tends to be slippery and dogs don't have good skid control, and because hard surfaces are tough on arthritic dog hips, area rugs with nonslip pads make a good safety—as well as décor—complement. For hiding, as well as repelling, dirt and stains, think dense, cut-pile wool or high-grade nylon in midrange colors. Patterns are your friends, too. Hemp, sisal, or seagrass weaves provide cover for light-haired shedders.

---

* *That's not true of vinyl flooring, for which it's sometimes mistaken. Vinyl uses lots of chemicals in its manufacturing—as opposed to linseed oil, a prime component of linoleum and the source of its name: Linum is Latin for flax, and linseed oil is derived from flaxseed.*

FURNITURE

Deterrence, especially through training, is the first line of defense in keeping your furniture safe from doggie depredations.

When you're at home ...

🦴   Be consistent. You can't decide that it's okay for your dog to sit next to you when you feel like having company on the couch and then yell at him when you don't. Firmly but pleasantly head your dog off when you see him approaching the verboten furniture, and direct him to get down if he's already settling in. Also ...

🦴   Provide alternatives. Guide your dog toward something else in the room such as a dog bed or less expensive piece of furniture.*

Techniques to train your pup from climbing on the furniture when you're away include:

🦴   Place wide swathes of masking tape, adhesive side up, on the furniture; it will stick to your dog's paws and/or fur and annoy him. Covering the cushions with aluminum foil will have a similarly irritating (though non-bonding) effect.

🦴   Rig up something noisy—a can full of coins, say—on the piece to startle your dog when he jumps on it.

🦴   Spray the furniture with something nontoxic but noxious to dogs, such as Bitter Apple.

The nice thing about these and similar techniques is that your dog won't associate you with these mildly aversive

---

* For example, that old beanbag chair from your hippie days that you could never bring yourself to throw away (unless your dog is a chewer; then you might actually find out what the chair is filled with). If, however, you redirect your dog to your significant other's favorite lounge chair, it would (correctly) be construed as a hostile act.

experiences and will instead resent the furniture. You should only need to use these measures temporarily, and not when you're expecting guests (unless they're the kind you would also like to discourage from settling in on your couch and armchairs).

COVER-UPS

Many of us don't mind sitting next to a warm body that doesn't try to commandeer the remote control, and don't view a mere species difference as sufficient reason to withhold a comfy snoozing spot. Washable throws* and slipcovers allow your dog furniture access without announcing your permissive policies to visitors.

Avoid throws with loose weaves that dogs can get their nails or collars caught on.

The following fabrics are particularly suited for slipcovers or upholstery:

- Linen and cotton blends. They're sturdy and launder well, and if you have a wrinkly dog, linen will provide the perfect fashion complement.

- Ultrasuede (www.ultrasuede.com). As with linoleum, this blast from the past has made a major comeback. It's pricey, but lush to the touch and stain resistant and machine washable. A quick sponging or brushing removes dog hair.

- Crypton (www.cryptonfabric.com). This similarly costly super fabric comes in several different textures and colors, all resistant to liquids, stains, and odors. Crypton's canine friendliness became a marketing strategy, when the company enlisted dog photographer William

---

*Or a facsimile thereof. My friend Karyn puts old sheets or blankets on the couch where her Greyhound, Lily, lounges. Because Karyn knows I'm not judgmental about dog-related untidiness—or untidiness in general—I'm not sure if the coverings are there for Lily's comfort or if they're removed before neater company arrives.

Wegman to design a fabric line. All the patterns feature dogs, and Wegman used his Weimeraners as models for the one called Posey.

As with rugs, think patterns and midtones for whatever type of fabric you opt for—or a color that's similar to your dog's hair. I noted in Chapter 1 that you are a bad person if you chose a dog to match your upholstery, but the converse doesn't hold true.

Finally, if you can afford it, consider leather furniture, which is easy to clean and disinfect. *One caveat:* If the leather doesn't have a finish, it will absorb oils from your dog's skin. Even if you never considered him a greaser, your pooch will slowly reveal his favorite place to relax by creating a full- or partial-body stain. Of course, this is another dog décor crisis where a stylish throw can come to the rescue.

87. WHAT'S THE BEST WAY TO CLEAN MY HOME NOW THAT I SHARE IT WITH A DOG?

This is a complex question, involving both effective methods of eliminating dog detritus and the need to avoid harming your pup with household cleaning products.

Frankie is lucky. I'm ecoconscious and not overly obsessed with cleanliness, so he isn't exposed to potentially toxic products on a regular basis. I in turn am fortunate to live with a nonshedding, housebroken pup. But we both have our lapses: I keep bleach in my dog-accessible laundry room, for example, and before Frankie was diagnosed and treated for diabetes, his excessive water consumption spurred a few accidents.

And, of course, feces happens.

DOG-DETRITUS CLEANUP

Most of the dog-related cleaning problems you'll encounter involve carpeting, which is why it's a good idea to get rid of the wall-to-wall variety if possible. Unless otherwise noted, the following deal with removing unwanted evidence of your pup's presence from your rug.

Liquid waste

The best way to eliminate urine stains and odor is to use a bacteria/enzyme digester, available from most pet stores as well as online. Make sure to use enough of the solution to penetrate your rug as deeply as the urine did, and take care to leave it on as long as directed. Keep your dog out of the room or put plastic over the area during this process. If your pup catches you removing his mark, he might up the pee ante.

For the same reason—as well as because of its potential toxicity—never use cleaning products that contain ammonia, also a prime component of urine. Your dog may think another dog snuck in and peed in his territory.

Speaking of sneaking, if your dog is a stealth urinater and you're not certain of the pee odor source, you can play CSI tech by searching the room with a black light. These lights usually cost less than $20; some even come free with odor removal products. If your baseboards and walls were targeted, mild soap and water should suffice to remove the evidence of your dog's misplaced machismo (sorry, but girl dogs don't tend to lift their legs to pee on the wall).

Semi-solid or solid waste

Waiting for complete solidification to occur is your best strategy. If you attempt to wash dog doo from your carpet before it dries, it will only smear and become embedded in the fibers.

To eliminate any odiferous flaky residue, add baking soda and then vacuum.

If the waste was semi-liquid to begin with or emerged from your dog's other end,* pick up and blot what you can with dry folded paper towels; be gentle so that you don't embed anything into the carpet. Once you remove the semi-solid portion, apply the same type of bacteria/enzyme digester you would use on urine. Or wait until the mess dries, sprinkle on baking soda, and vacuum.

Hair

The best dog hair defense is a good offense (or is that the other way around? I get my sports metaphors confused): the more frequently you groom your dog, the less hair will be arrayed around your house. But, even more than feces, shed happens, and it's impossible to avoid furry furnishings if you live with a breed that has a nonstick coat. The solution: vacuum, vacuum, vacuum. Vacuum cleaner manufacturers have risen to the occasion, creating a mind-boggling array of products and attachments aimed at those beset by pet hair.** Among them are robotic vacuums, which not only do the job without human effort but, because they beep and flash, inspire some dogs to believe they're exciting toys intended for them. Any possible benefits of this illusion, of course, depend on how your dog treats her playthings. Indeed, some dogs mistake robotic vacuums for aliens that need to be attacked and sent back to space.

---

* Yes, we're discussing vomit and diarrhea. If you don't get to the former quickly, your dog may resolve part of the problem by eating what he's just upchucked. I was shocked when I first saw my refined little Frankie recycle his discarded food, but I guess he wasn't going to let a little gastric acid keep him from enjoying something he liked the first time around.

** Consumer Reports often tests vacuum cleaners for their effectiveness in dealing with pet hair. The 81-model survey published in 2008 made owners of Dyson models, which weren't very highly rated, very irate. They rushed to the defense of their preferred brand on various Internet forums.

In addition, as with dried dog poop and vomit, baking soda makes a great vacuuming aid, bonding to hair, bacteria, and dander; it also helps eliminate doggie odor. Sprinkle it on and let it sit for about half an hour before suctioning it up.

DO-NO-HARM CLEANING

Imagine a toddler being allowed to crawl all around the house, licking the floor at will. Then imagine that she has a super-fast metabolism and smaller-than-human lung capacity. That's your dog's MO—which means she's not only at increased risk of encountering household cleaning toxins, but that when she does, she's breathing them in more rapidly than we do and having more difficulty eliminating them from her body.

Surprise! The best way to prevent your dog from being exposed to dangerous chemicals is to avoid using products that contain them. The most common offenders and cleaners in which they're found include:

Ammonia: Glass cleaners (combined with bleach, ammonia creates a poisonous chlorine gas)

Bleach: Disinfectants and clothes whiteners

Formaldehyde: Furniture polish

Monoethanolamine: Oven, tub, tile, and carpet cleaners

Turpentine: Furniture polishes

Phosphoric acid: Liquid dishwasher detergents and bathroom cleaning products, especially those used on mildew and lime

Not the type to mix vinegar, baking soda, peroxide, and salt to create your own safe cleaning solution? No problem. Green cleaning is in, even with the major manufacturers.

It's easy to find environment-friendly, nontoxic substitutes to tackle every area of your home that needs attention.

If you're convinced you can't find something that works as well as an unsafe product, make sure to keep your dog away from those surfaces until they're completely dry.

Of course, you're not going to be able to divest your house of everything that's potentially dangerous to your dog. In its animal poison control list, the ASPCA (aspca.org; click "Pet Care" and "Animal Poison Control") warns against everything from cold medications to post-1982 pennies.

The bottom line is to get rid of what you can, minimize exposure to what you won't, and store the rest in a safe, inaccessible place. Also keep the number of your vet and the ASPCA Animal Poison Control Center's 24-hour hotline handy: 1-888-426-4435.

88. WHICH PLANTS ARE SAFE TO HAVE AROUND MY DOG?

This question is predicated on the reasonable assumption that at some point your dog will have an urge to eat something vegetal that's not on his regular menu. Frankie is particularly fond of grass, in spite—or perhaps because—of the fact that it tends to make him throw up.

Puke-inducement notwithstanding, munching grass doesn't present a health problem, but you'd be amazed at how many seemingly benign flowers and plants can (at minimum) cause more serious stomach upset, and (at maximum) be fatal. The ASPCA puts amaryllis, azaleas, chrysanthemums, cyclamen, English ivy, oleanders, pothos, rhododendrons, schefflera, and tulips on its top offenders list.* See www. aspca.org (under "Pet Care," "Animal Poison Control," and "Toxic Plants") for the complete list of 17 Common Poisonous Plants, as well as for the more comprehensive lists of plants to avoid and plants to plant.

Of course, even the most benign plants can be rendered dangerous with the use of chemical herbicides, insecticides, and pesticides. Among the most toxic are those containing methomyl, metaldehyde, disyston or disulfoton, and zinc phosphide.

Nonchemical fertilizers are generally dog friendly—with important exceptions. Cocoa bean mulch, for example, contains, well, cocoa beans, and thus theobromine and caffeine—the same ingredients that make brownies verboten to dogs.

---

* *Marijuana makes this short list, too, so keep your dog out of the grow room and don't let her get into any pot brownies (a double threat because chocolate is bad for her health, too). Ingestion is the only form of cannabis contact that the ASPCA warns against, but your pup should be discouraged from smoking weed because it's illegal.*

I was about to suggest things you could do to minimize the hazards if you insist on using chemicals in your yard, but it occurred to me that any toxins you use will inevitably infiltrate the water supply. If you want to be a bad global citizen, let someone else be an enabler; I'm not going to tell you how to poison me and Frankie.

89. IS THERE A WAY TO KEEP MY DOG FROM DIGGING UP MY GARDEN?

Probably—but first you need to dig into your dog's psyche to get at the source of her underground urges.

A great deal of tunneling is breed related. Terriers, for example, live to search and destroy prey, the more deeply embedded the better, while furry northern breeds like Siberian Huskies try to escape the heat by creating underground shelters. But some types of digging transcend genes (if not always gender). Unneutered males—especially those with strong noses—dig to get out of Dodge and hit on girls in heat, and pups of every variety move dirt around to escape boredom.

Finding the source of the digging urge can help you figure out whether to try to eliminate or redirect it.

Keeping your Siberia-bound digger indoors at the hottest time of day or during the warmest months, for example, might suffice to eliminate his excavations, while providing chew toys, especially food-oriented ones, could alleviate boredom (see Chapter 7 for other entertainment options).

And you can either keep your flowerbeds or your male dog intact.

If you have a terrier or other natural tunneler, however, diversion is probably the best tactic. *To wit:* Give your dog her own personal digging pit.

Pick out a corner, loosen the soil and/or add sand, and set up barriers—not high enough to prevent access, but clear enough to provide boundaries. Then lure your dog to the area by burying toys, food, or whatever treasure you think she would want to unearth. If your pup doesn't have an especially strong sniffer, let her watch the process. It might take a bit of time to establish your garden's dog patch, but eventually you'll create a gardening companion who's not Shiva the destroyer.

And don't forget to replenish the dirt and underground goodies now and then to maintain the desirability of this bit of doggie real estate.

CHAPTER 10

LOOSE ENDS—AND ENDINGS

90. AM I USING MY DOG AS A SUBSTITUTE FOR MY KIDS WHO LEFT FOR COLLEGE?

Yes. And why do you think this is a problem?

When did your children last take long walks with you, listen to you without interrupting to ask for money, and fail to criticize your clothing choices?

With a dog, your unconditional love will be requited.*

Only the very unlucky would have their dogs run away and their adult children return home to live with them.

Your relationship with your dog might even improve your relationship with any irritating, overly demanding offspring. When you see said ingrates, just keep referring positively to Leona Helmsley, who willed $12 million** to her Maltese, Trouble, while leaving two of her four grandchildren bupkus. Your own relatives should get the hint—and if they don't, they're too thick to be fiscally responsible and will doubtless squander your hard-earned money.

And at least you can say you've been there, done that as far as producing progeny is concerned. Some people worry that getting a dog is a substitute for having children. To them I say the world is greatly overpopulated. You're helping to conserve the earth's limited resources. And if you rescued and spayed or neutered your dog, you earned double the good karma points. (If, on the other hand, you supported a puppy mill,

---

* *Unconditional shouldn't be confused with constant or uninterrupted, however. An interest in food, for example, might distract even the most affectionate of dogs from adoration duty. But dogs don't hold grudges, so you won't experience more than a temporary withholding of affection if, say, you don't deliver dinner in a timely fashion.*

** *A Manhattan judge reduced Trouble's bequest to a mere $2 million after the family contested the will on the grounds that Helmsley was not of sound mind when she wrote it. Be sure to emphasize the unfairness of that decision—in a very lucid fashion. And note that the uncontested bulk of Helmsley's fortune, several billion dollars, was left to animal care charities.*

points will be deducted. I'm not sure how many; the universe rarely speaks to me in specifics.)

And there are those who fear they've gotten a dog to avoid relationships with other people entirely. No worries. Human and canine bonds are far from mutually exclusive. Unless your pup tries to bite everyone he comes into contact with—in which case a lot more training is in order—a dog usually serves as a social lubricant.

That said, human relationships tend to be overrated. And at least with a dog, you're bound to get more fresh air and exercise than you would if you were parked at your computer buying power tools for your Second Life avatar.

91. WHAT SHOULD I SAY TO PEOPLE WHO CRITICIZE ME FOR SPENDING TOO MUCH ON MY DOG?

It's one of life's oddities. Few people would question your purchase of a flat-screen TV or of a new car—unless you couldn't afford it, in which case, under the guise of concern, your friends and family members would discuss your spendthrift ways behind your back. But many will feel free to second-guess the amount you spend on a living creature who gives you great joy (and doesn't question your purchases, unless you've bought the wrong type of dog food).

Responses to their criticism might include:

- Questioning some of their recent purchases for their children/significant others, noting that your dog is smarter and more grateful (not recommended, but fun to contemplate).

- Inquiring how much they spent on their shoes/jacket/ last restaurant dinner—anything that might be expensive—and asking if the money wouldn't be better directed toward [fill in the name of a charity or political cause]. If your interlocutors are not given to costly or frivolous purchases and do give money to [fill in the name of a charity or political cause], you can inquire how much they've given to animal welfare lately. (Don't worry; if animal welfare was one of their causes, they never would have questioned your canine-directed expenditures.)

But this brings up a valid issue of priorities. You might consider donating some money to dogs in need* instead of buying yours a new collar; dogs don't much care what they wear. If you're flush enough to do both, more power to you.** Then again, it's really none of my business—which is the best answer (in reverse) you can give anyone who questions your spending habits.

92. I'D LIKE TO BRING MY DOG TO WORK. HOW CAN I FIND A DOG-FRIENDLY JOB?

I included this question in my book outline before the economy began tanking, and—given the current difficulty of finding work, period—thought about substituting something else. Then it occurred to me that the dog/job question was still very relevant. Involuntarily becoming a freelancer, independent contractor, or plain old unemployed person allows you to spend more time with your dog—a perk that inspired many a boom-time decision to telecommute, whether publicly acknowledged or not.†

---

* If you need help deciding on a reputable charity, see petplace.com/dogs/tip-on-choosing-a-pet-charity-for-dogs/page1.aspx.

** And Frankie wants to know, can I get a loan?

† In most business circles, it's still more acceptable to say, "I want to stay home with my children" than to assert, "My dog really needs me during this crucial furniture-chewing phase."

And the dog-friendly workplace is not just a bark in the dark; it's likely to be around for a long time. Nearly one in five businesses—most of them smaller or nontraditional (like Google)—allow dogs on the premises, a policy that has little to do with benevolence. Studies show that welcoming pets* increases productivity and reduces absenteeism. Some 66 percent of respondents to a Dogster.com survey said they would work longer hours if they had their dogs with them; 49 percent said they would switch jobs if they could take their dog to work; 32 percent said they'd take a pay cut to work with their dogs; and 70 percent considered a dog-friendly workplace an important employee benefit.

Thus, in lieu of cash bonuses, paid health care, and other more conventional perks that workers became accustomed to in the pretanked economy, welcoming dogs is an inexpensive way for employers to show their love. If you run a business

---

* *This theoretically includes the likes of cats and birds, but "pet-friendly" is a nonspeciesist euphemism for what is overwhelmingly an open-dog policy.*

and want to attract canine-keen talent, get hold of *Dogs at Work* by Liz Palika and Jennifer Fearing. Published by the Humane Society of the United States, this book not only lays out convincing arguments for the advantages of enacting dog-friendly policies but also provides step-by-step advice on how to do so effectively.

For employees, the benefits of a dog-friendly workplace are greater than just being able to hang out with your pup; you'll also have an in with upper management. Companies usually put out the animal welcome mat because the CEOs want their own dogs around. Legally, employers can't avoid hiring people with dog allergies, phobias, and plain old dislikes (go figure), and their canine concerns have to be addressed. Such people might even have useful skills. But employees who can praise the boss's pooch with genuine enthusiasm,* or recommend the latest healthy kibble, have a definite advantage.

Jobs for those who don't want to suffer dog separation anxiety continue to be listed on DogFriendly.com (find the "workplace" area) as well as on such standard sites as simplyhired.com and monster.com. No bites? Commercial real estate is going for a song. This might be the perfect time for you to start your own pooch-friendly enterprise with other top talent that's been let off a company's leash.

93. I'D LIKE TO PUT MY DOG TO WORK. HOW DO I GO ABOUT DOING THAT?

As with the previous question, the economic downturn gave this a different slant than I had originally intended. I meant to address only canine volunteer work such as visiting old

---

* It's possible, of course, for the boss to have an unruly and thus annoying dog, but every dog lover knows where the blame lies in that case.

age homes or helping kids read.* But a November 2008 segment of Animal Planet's *Dogs 101* has turned out to be very timely. It featured a Beagle named Tracer who is gainfully employed sniffing out bedbug infestations. Tracer and his pal Ace, a Beagle-Husky mix, help Mike Tache, the owner of American K-9 Investigators Pest Control, earn up to $200 an hour.

Perhaps your dog also does something marketable. And, no, being cute doesn't count—except for dog actors and models, but their ability to take direction is far more important.

If your dog specializes in restrained friendliness, however, she might very well be suited for a nonprofit position. When it comes to visiting hospitals and other public service jobs, temperament is far more important than good looks or even talent. Although Frankie is cute as all get out, for example, and extremely bright, he doesn't cozy up to strangers—or friends, for that matter. Several have mentioned feeling rejected by Frankie's failure to welcome them, no matter how many times they've been to my house. Imagine the effect on a sick person of a small-dog shunning.

To find out if your dog is suited for a healing profession, click on the "Activities" and then "Therapy" section of DogPlay. com. The website not only lists many local and national organizations that can help evaluate your dog and find him a job if he passes muster, but also clears up the confusion surrounding the use of such terms as "visiting dog," "therapy dog," and "animal-assisted activity" (these generally refer to volunteer programs geared toward groups) and "animal assisted therapy" (most often used for professional programs tailored to individuals).

---

* *Honest. After-school programs around the country proved that reading to a furry, nonjudgmental audience improves children's skills. The dogs, of course, sharpen their listening skills and expand their vocabularies.*

94. DO ALL DOGS GET GRUMPY WHEN THEY GET OLD?

That question makes *me* grumpy, and I'm not even that old. It's not age that makes geriatric dogs—and people—irritable but, rather, untreated pain and undiagnosed ailments. Your pup might have arthritis, for example, or hearing problems that you're not aware of. And now that modern veterinary science is helping dogs live longer, a version of Alzheimer's called canine cognitive dysfunction (CCD, or sometimes CDS for cognitive dysfunction syndrome) has become more common. CCD causes disorientation in dogs, just as Alzheimer's does in humans.

So if your dog isn't her usual cheerful, goofy self, get her to the vet to see what's wrong. Whether or not there's a cure, you can make her life easier after you know what you're dealing with. If your dog has hearing loss, for example, you can move into her line of vision when you need to get her attention; if she has CCD, you can refrain from rearranging the furniture and thus further confusing her. And veterinary pain management has also advanced in recent years—including the recognition that alternative treatments like acupuncture may be better for older dogs on a long-term basis than harsh medicines.

See also the following question about dietary and exercise changes.

95. SHOULD I CHANGE MY DOG'S DIET AND CUT BACK ON HER EXERCISE WHEN SHE GETS OLDER?

It depends; you're as likely to want to cut back on your dog's diet and change her exercise as vice versa. And "older" is as much of a relative term for dogs as it is for humans (ask any baby boomer). Whereas large breeds start being offered seats on public transportation at age 6 or so, smaller ones don't begin reminiscing about the good old days until they're around 10 or 11. And some dogs don't conform to ageist stereotypes: they continue to eat and exercise with much the same gusto as they did when they were pups. The following, then, are just general guidelines.

DIET

When your dog's metabolism begins to slow, he'll need to cut calories or eat less to stay trim. Extra weight puts a strain on the joints—especially painful if arthritis is involved—and often interferes with proper organ function.

Older pooches need a good balance of protein and fat in their diet, but don't require as much of either as they did when they were burning up the dog run. The key to fooling your dog into thinking she's full is fiber—also a useful antidote for that common geriatric ailment, constipation. Many older dogs can continue to eat their regular food, just less of it—perhaps with pumpkin added for low fat/high fiber bulk.

Some canine seniors have the opposite problem: they lose interest in food. It's not always easy to figure out why. Your dog may be avoiding his kibble because the pieces are too large for her to chew comfortably any more, or because, with her sense of smell diminished, she's begun finding the cuisine incredibly bland. You'll need to experiment. Try a smaller size kibble, for example, or soak the one you've been using in low-salt meat broth. Or switch from kibble to an entirely different type of food, such as canned, freeze-dried, or home-cooked; this last may be especially beneficial if your dog is having gastrointestinal problems and needs easy-to-digest fare such as chicken and rice. See Chapter 4 for suggestions about getting the nutritional balance right.

EXERCISE

Let your dog set the pace when it comes to cutting back (or not) on workouts, although not to the point of allowing him to over- or under-do it. Dogs can sometimes push themselves too hard, especially in extreme weather, or take retirement a bit too seriously. Neither approach benefits their physical or mental health.

A change, rather than reduction, in exercise might be a good idea. You could try easier-on-the-joint activities such as swimming, for example (only an option if your dog doesn't dislike full-body immersion as much as Frankie does). And if you need to cut back on a standard play routine, consider allowing your dog to think she's as agile as ever by not throwing the ball as far as you used to.*

Mental exercise is also essential to maintaining a puppyish demeanor. A much-cited Beagle study—well, much cited in neurobiology circles, and not to be confused with the studies Charles Darwin conducted while aboard the *H.M.S. Beagle*—demonstrated that aging dogs who received mental stimulation, along with antioxidant-enriched diets, appeared friskier and smarter than the nonstimulated, nonsupplemented control group after two years. So keep up the training, play dates, educational toys, *New York Times* crossword puzzles ... whatever challenges your dog.

96. WHAT IF SOMETHING HAPPENS TO ME AND I CAN'T TAKE CARE OF MY DOG?

In some ways, this situation is harder to deal with than the usual order of things, i.e., your dog departing the world

---

* *Oh, like you've never done anything to salve your dog's ego. After I had the vet pull several of Frankie's teeth, I made him believe the ones he had left had become much stronger by pretending I could no longer pull his squeaky chile toy out of his mouth. At least I think he believes that. For all I know, he could just be playing along to assuage my guilt over his drastic—albeit essential to his health—de-toothing.*

before you do. For one thing, you're forced to consider the future of your poor bereft pup whom no one will ever love as much as you do. For another, you have to contemplate your own incapacitation and demise. Perhaps worst of all, you'll need to complete a great deal of legal paperwork. So have a beer or three, wallow for a bit—and then get off your butt. Your dog will be far more bereft if she ends up at the pound because you didn't arrange for her care.

Among the contingencies to consider: being downed for a few days or weeks; being laid up for an indefinite period of time; and being put out of commission permanently. With children, the urgency of ensuring a smooth handover to a designated guardian is always recognized. That's not the case with dogs, considered property in the eyes of the law. But your dog can't wait in a safety deposit box for a will to be probated—and you can't assume that, because your good pal Dave has always liked your pup, he'll be pleased to take permanent custody. The first order of business, then, is to remove the elements of delay and surprise from any arrangements you make.

In the following sections, I've outlined some possible scenarios and solutions. The comprehensive "Providing for Your Pet's Future Without You" section of the Humane Society's website (hsus.org/petsinwills) goes into greater detail. But it's essential that you find an attorney—preferably one with a dog—who knows the laws regarding pet dispensation in your state (see also the following question).

One way to streamline the process of reaching your emergency contacts is PetLifeline, a service offered by PetsMobility (petsmobility.com) for about $40 a year. You give the company detailed information about how to locate your dog's designated guardian, and in turn receive cards and key tags with the company's number. PetLifeline's services include not only locating a guardian and ensuring that he or she actually retrieves your dog but also following up in a week or so to see how your dog (and you) are doing. Thus anyone who is busy rescuing you or grieving over you only has to make a single phone call—and has no excuse for ignoring your dog because a caretaker couldn't easily be found.

SHORT-TERM

Making an arrangement for a temporary guardian for your dog shouldn't be too difficult. It can be done informally, although not without forethought. A key concern is making your wishes known if you're unable to talk. If you don't want to use a formal service like PetLifeline, keep a typed—or at least legible—card in your wallet and car noting the existence of your dog and providing contact information for your designated emergency caretaker(s).

Of course, it's essential to find friends or relatives—plural, because you need a contingency caretaker in case the primary is unavailable—who like dogs in general and yours in particular.* Make sure the people you choose agree to take on the responsibility, and then give them keys to your house, instructions about the care and feeding of your dog, and contact information for your vet.

You can also specify a professional arrangement, such as having your dog brought over to the place where you board him when you go on vacation. Frankie's diabetes and his dislike of leaving his domain rule out a caretaker who doesn't know how to give injections—as well as a stay away from home. Therefore, along with my keys, I gave two trusted friends a list of the reliable, insulin-savvy dogsitters I've used in the past.

---

* *He or she doesn't necessarily have to like you, however. No matter how annoying you are, a dog lover would not want harm to come to your canine charge. Another thing that favors compliance: any temporary guardian is bound to be aware that you'll be back in action sooner or later, owing them big time (karmically, if not financially).*

LONG-TERM OR PERMANENT

Two rules to ensure that your dog will be cared for in case of your long-time distraction or demise: put it in writing and put your money where your mouth is. The best of intentions can't prevent informal arrangements, even those promising remuneration, from falling apart. In contrast, a will or trust that clarifies a caretaker's responsibilities and specifies compensation is harder to wiggle out of.

Of course, there are no guarantees of compliance if circumstances change, so keep in close touch with your designated guardian. My best friend, Clare, agreed long ago to take Frankie in if anything should happen to me, but after he was diagnosed with diabetes I asked her again. She assured me that nothing had changed, and I believe her. It doesn't hurt that Clare is the executor of my estate and therefore will be in charge of my money, and that, although she is the most lapsed Catholic I know, she's aware that she will go to hell if Frankie should be made unhappy.*

97. HOW CAN I LEARN ABOUT OTHER LEGAL ISSUES SURROUNDING MY DOG?

Ah, yes—your dog bites, or gets bitten; you want custody of your pup when you and your spouse split; or you think your neighbor should fix the hole on his side of the fence so your dog can't escape ... A good place to start learning about your rights—or lack thereof—is *Every Dog's Legal Guide* by Mary Randolph. After you get a general sense of what's covered by

---

* *Speaking of which, if you're convinced that your dog will be so distraught when you die that he needs to be euthanized, and you include a clause to that effect in your will, there's a good chance that it will not stand up in court. And that you will go to hell. If you live in one of the 37 states that allow for the establishment of a pet trust, this is your best option. It eliminates the need to wait until your will is probated for the guardianship arrangement to take effect. A living trust might be even better, as it allows you to arrange for the guardianship to kick in before you kick off (say, if you're in a coma for more than a month).*

the legal system, and how, log on to animallaw.com. There you can search your state's statutes—or lack thereof—on specific issues. Animallaw.com also offers useful links to other sites that focus on animal legalities.

That doesn't mean you shouldn't use an attorney if you want to go to court. In fact, if you live in California, I suggest you hire my friend Clare.*

98. HOW DO I KNOW WHEN "IT'S TIME"—AND WHAT DO I DO WHEN I'VE DECIDED?

It's ironic that we're often forced to make end-of-life decisions for dogs, who can't tell us what they want, but are prevented from carrying out the wishes of humans, who can. But if we're powerless to design the deaths we might desire for ourselves and for our human loved ones, we can provide them for our pups, shielding them from prolonged pain and suffering. Dogs in turn have the advantage of living in the present, so they don't anticipate and fear the end in the same way we do (or at least they don't write turgid novels or make pretentious movies about it).

I only hope someone gives me the type of sendoff my friend Karyn's Greyhound, Painter, got. When he was 11 years old, Painter developed spinal deterioration to the point that he could barely walk. When he crouched to go to the bathroom, he had trouble lifting himself back up. Unable to carry around a 75-pound Greyhound and distraught to see him losing his dignity, Karyn finally called the vet to come over and give him an injection.

The day of the appointment, Karyn was too upset to think about preparing food, so I brought over a couple of burritos for us, a bacon cheeseburger for Painter. "He can't eat that,"

---

* *Ignore this suggestion if I'm no longer alive, because Clare will then need to devote all her time to ensuring Frankie's happiness.*

Karyn started to protest when she saw the burger, "He has pancreatitis." Then she remembered. "Well," she amended, "he hasn't had much appetite, but let's try it." Sure enough, Painter perked right up, scarfing the burger in three bites. Afterward, he farted contentedly in Karyn's arms until the vet arrived half an hour later.

Just as you're the only one who can decide when the balance has tipped from mild discomfort to suffering for your dog— and from manageable expense to deep debt for yourself*— the decision about where to say goodbye is extremely personal. For me, familiar surroundings—as opposed to a medical facility—seem the least stressful. If your vet won't make a final house call, you should be able to find one who will. Some will even accompany you to a beach, woods, or other place your dog loves. That said, many clinics have separate, hospicelike areas where euthanizations are done, so you won't have to sit sobbing in a room with a bunch of happy puppies waiting for vaccinations. And that way you won't associate your home or a favorite spot with a sad memory.

As for the final arrangements, most vets will also take care of cremation or transfer to a pet cemetery. Or a human cemetery. A bill passed in Florida, for example, permits pet ashes to be placed inside an owner's casket so long as they're in a separate urn. Some human cemeteries have separate pet areas—often a better bet than a dedicated pet cemetery, which is not always protected by law and can be turned into a strip mall if the owner sells the land. Check your local ordinances, including those on backyard burials; they're often prohibited, but the pet interment police rarely go out on patrol.

---

* *If you're reading this while your dog is still young, a reminder about health insurance: don't leave your dog without it. But just because insurance provides the means for you to prolong your dog's life, doing so is not necessarily in her best interest.*

Painter, incidentally, rests in a lovely raku urn on Karyn's desk, where he helps inspire her continued and tireless efforts on behalf of Greyhound rescue.

99. WHAT IS THE RAINBOW BRIDGE—AND DO ALL DOGS GO THERE?

A catchall term for pet heaven, the multicolor span debuted in 1997 in Paul C. Dahm's "The Legend of the Rainbow Bridge." According to the story, every cherished pet that dies goes to live in a verdant meadow below the bridge, restored to youth and health, eating delicious food, and cavorting happily with other pets. The only thing missing from the picture is the beloved human companion: you. When you arrive, there is great celebration and then you cross over together to the other side.

I confess that I cry like a baby whenever I read this story. It's only after I blow my nose that I start nitpicking the details—as I do with all strict delineations of the hereafter.

Meadows are all well and good, I think, but shouldn't spilled garbage, a dog favorite through the ages, be involved, too? And pigs' ears? If so, would pet pigs get a separate area to wait for their ascent to hog heaven, one where dogs won't covet their hearing organs? And, as I mentioned in this book's introduction, my mother feared all creatures great and small. Did she shed her animal anxieties when she left her body—or will I be forced to choose between hanging out with her or Frankie? (Don't ask.)

And what about dogs who don't have loving owners to help them cross over? They deserve happiness, too—even more so than those who had it on Earth. If I were designing an after-life, those pups would go to the other side as soon as the person who mistreated or abandoned them died. Said offender would be transformed into a slab of bacon and spend eternity being gnawed on by the dog(s) he or she wronged. (What can I say? I grew up with a vengeful deity—and with cravings for forbidden pork products.)

100. HOW SHOULD I RESPOND TO PEOPLE WHO TELL ME, "IT WAS ONLY A DOG" AND THAT I'M GRIEVING TOO LONG?

You shouldn't respond at all, at least not if you want these people in your life in some capacity.* It will be extremely tempting to offer an equally insensitive rejoinder, and that can only lead to insult escalation. Just file the remark away with all the other hurtful comments you'll likely receive, and then haul it out to be mocked by members of your pet grief support group or informal network of dog lovers who under-stand what you're going through. The person on duty at the

---

* If you're certain you won't need and/or are unlikely ever to encounter these people again, saying very bad words, including a command to attempt the anatomically impossible, is an excellent option.

ASPCA's Pet Loss Hotline (1-877-474-3310) should be able to talk you down, too.

If you're not a joiner or generally dislike sharing, consider a personalized dartboard, punching bag, or other inanimate target toward which you can channel your anger. Cheek turning apparently works for some people, too, although not for those with whom I tend to socialize.

Above all, don't take comments like these to heart. Grieve as long as you need to and when you're ready—but only then—get another dog. He'll never replace the one you've lost but will enrich your life in his own inimitable doggy fashion.